THE EXAMPLE OF RICHARD WRIGHT

DAN McCALL

THE

EXAMPLE

of

RICHARD

WRIGHT

Harcourt, Brace & World, Inc., New York

The quotations from Richard Wright's *Native Son*
(Harper, 1940) and *Black Boy* (Harper, 1945)
are reprinted by permission of Harper &
Row, Publishers. The excerpt from his *Lawd Today*,
copyright © 1963 by Ellen Wright, is used by permission
of Walker & Co., New York, and of Anthony Blond Ltd.,
London (British and Commonwealth edition). The poem
by Conrad Kent Rivers "To Richard Wright" was first
published in the *Antioch Review*, Volume XX, Number
4, and is used by permission of that journal.

Library of Congress Catalog Card Number: 69-14837
Printed in the United States of America

To the memory of

MELVIN TOLSON

ACKNOWLEDGMENTS

I owe much to the scholars, students, and friends who have directed my thinking and offered helpful suggestions. Special thanks to Stephen Donadio, Oscar and Sarah Lumpkin, Constance Webb, Reuben Munday, and Sarah Diamant.

I am indebted to Keneth Kinnamon's unpublished doctoral thesis, "The Emergence of Richard Wright: A Literary, Biographical, and Social Study" (Harvard, 1966), for the quotation from James Kimble Vardaman and for the story of the lynching used on page 6.

My wife, Dorothy, is my best critic and sustaining presence.

D. McC.

CONTENTS

"The greatest defeat, in anything, is to forget, and above all to forget what it is that has smashed you, and to let yourself be smashed without ever realizing how thoroughly devilish men can be. When our time is up, we people mustn't bear malice, but neither must we forget: we must tell the whole thing, without altering one word, —everything that we have seen of man's viciousness; and then it will be over and time to go. That is enough of a job for a whole lifetime."

LOUIS-FERDINAND CÉLINE
Journey to the End of Night

THE EXAMPLE OF RICHARD WRIGHT

CHAPTER 1

"Ah Feels It in Mah Bones"

In March of 1954 Galion, Ohio, removed
Native Son from its high-school library.
This action was part of the city's American-
ism program, which included an anti-Com-
munist loyalty oath for the public-school
teachers. A Board of Education member
made a statement, printed in the Galion
Inquirer (March 11), in which he suggested
that they should not "burn" *Native Son;*
instead, the librarian should "acquire other
books honestly telling of negro life with
less raw bitterness."

A central problem in Richard Wright's
work, and in our understanding of it, is the
nature of the relationship between raw bitterness and honest telling. In a literary
journal one critic has complained that in
Native Son "the South, lynch mobs, the

yellow press" are treated "in exaggerated ridicule" and the "actual circumstances, without any distortion, can present a more convincing and terrifying story." That objection seems justified. When we look back, now, on that story of South Side Chicago in the late thirties we think we see cartoons. After Bigger Thomas has been brought to the inquest, Wright concocts a newspaper account that seems like parody, grotesquely exaggerated satire of American race prejudice:

Though the Negro killer's body does not seem compactly built, he gives the impression of possessing abnormal physical strength. He is about five feet, nine inches tall and his skin is exceedingly black. His lower jaw protrudes obnoxiously, reminding one of a jungle beast.

His arms are long, hanging in a dangling fashion to his knees. It is easy to imagine how this man, in the grip of a brain-numbing sex passion, overpowered little Mary Dalton, raped her, murdered her, beheaded her, then stuffed her body into a roaring furnace to destroy the evidence of his crime.

His shoulders are huge, muscular, and he keeps them hunched, as if about to spring upon you at any moment. He looks at the world with a strange, sullen, fixed-from-under stare, as though defying all efforts of compassion.

All in all, he seems a beast utterly untouched by the softening influences of modern civilization. In speech and manner he lacks the charm of the average, harmless, genial, grinning southern darky so beloved by the American people.

The moment the killer made his appearance at the inquest, there were shouts of "Lynch 'im! Kill 'im!"

But the brutish Negro seemed indifferent to his fate, as though inquests, trials, and even the looming certainty of the electric chair held no terror for him. He acted like an earlier missing link in the human species.

While Wright was working on *Native Son,* a case broke in Chicago that was remarkably similar to the fiction he was in the process of mapping out. In late May of 1938, a Negro boy of eighteen, Robert Nixon, was apprehended for the slaying of Florence Johnson, a fireman's wife. While she was at home, while her husband was out serving the city, the Negro "moron" (as he was called on the back page of the Chicago *Daily Tribune*, May 28) got her. Chicago had been enduring a two-year wave of "sex moron" crimes, fourteen victims. When Nixon and his "accomplice," a boy named Hicks, went to re-enact the crime at the Johnson place, they were menaced, according to the *Tribune*, by a hundred neighbors crying, "Why don't they lynch them?" Back at the jail Nixon only "wolfed his favorite fare—four bottles of pop and three pieces of cocoanut pie—with relish" (*Tribune*, May 30). A report was sent north from the sheriff of Nixon's hometown in Louisiana; the sheriff said the boy "had been on the prowl since he was six" and "nothing but death will cure him." The police had been working on Nixon; by June 3 the *Tribune* front page had the headline, "Science Traps Moron in 5 Murders." And two days later "The World's Greatest Newspaper" described him as a "jungle beast," noting that "ferocity is reflected in Nixon's features" and providing on page six the words of a cop who watched him climb the fire escapes to re-enact the crime: "Look at him go, just like an ape." Although the "ape" had come from "a pretty little town in the old South" he had "none of the charm of speech or manner that is characteristic of so many Southern darkies." The *Tribune* speaks (June 5):

That charm is a mark of civilization, and so far as manner and appearance go, civilization has left Nixon practically untouched. His hunched shoulders and long sinewy arms that dangle almost to his knees; his outthrust head and catlike tread all suggest the animal.

He is very black—almost pure Negro. His physical characteristics suggest an earlier link in the species.

Having built this pretrial cage around the "jungle Negro"— the "almost pure Negro"—the *Tribune* then nails a warning

on the bars: "though docile enough under ordinary circumstances, they are easily aroused."

In *Native Son* Wright does not indulge his capacity for
inventing cartoons. If, as is so frequently objected, *Native
Son* deals with cartoons, Richard Wright did not draw them
out of his imagination. White America beat him to that.

He was born September 4, 1908, on a plantation twenty-
five miles from Natchez; the governor of Mississippi that
year was James Kimble Vardaman, the "Great White Chief,"
who distinguished himself by such public proclamations as
"The way to control the nigger is to whip him when he
does not obey without it, and another is never to pay him
more wages than is actually necessary to buy food and cloth-
ing." In his migratory childhood Wright knew Memphis.
When he was nine, a Negro was lynched five miles outside
the city limits by a mob of 5,000; the black man was burned
alive, his heart was cut out, and he was then dismembered.
The head and a leg were propped up on Beale Street and a
white barbershop sought to attract customers by a souvenir
of the body.

How does one write about such a world, and how is it to
be "interpreted" in literary art? Wright's first book, *Uncle
Tom's Children,* a collection of four novellas about race and
violence in the South, was published in 1938; all his major
work was done by 1945. He was writing before the Civil
Rights Movement, writing to an audience that had little
sense of "the Negro" in America other than what could
be acquired in small talk with the maid or chauffeur or a
Saturday night in "Darktown"—little sense of "the Problem" other than the clichés that made hot copy for the Chicago *Tribune* in the Nixon case. Without any Movement
to bring the black man's dilemma to our attention, Richard
Wright often felt he was going it alone. That solitary journey
took an immense toll of his resources, and in 1946 he sought

release from the pain by choosing exile in France. He stayed there until his death, fourteen years later.

He cannot be considered without a sense of uneasy desperation. His voice is a single one, that of a lonely, furious, proud black man from the South, telling us that our culture is crazy. And the more he cries *White Man, Listen!* (the title of one of his nonfiction books) the clearer it becomes to him that the White Man will not listen and does not want to. You can see it getting to Wright—the sense of exhaustion, futility in protest, the utter abject weariness; he cannot hold his hands up but he reels with his conviction that the country must be punched awake, must be guided through the sewers of its racial sickness.

He wrote in *Black Boy*: "That was the way things were between whites and blacks in the South; many of the most important things were never openly said; they were understated and left to seep through to one." In his own writing he rarely operates on that principle: he does not understate; he drives his irony like a truck, and "the most important things" are presented over and over, underlined, and rarely left to "seep through to one." His prose is hurried, often inattentive; he gives the impression of a man who has been forced so long to keep silent that when he finally opens his mouth to speak to us he cannot talk, he must burst. In many ways he felt himself to be what the white reviewers kept calling him: Spokesman for the Negro People.

While the responsibilities of such a "spokesman" are large, they also limit his continuing importance and the nature of his statement. The demands of public utterance are not usually friendly to the success of art. As times change we need new spokesmen. And several critics have suggested that the work of Richard Wright is less than helpful where the Civil Rights Movement has become history and the "American dilemma" entails a reckoning with Black Power.

Richard Wright is, in one commentator's words, merely "a historical and sociological document." He works in close with stereotypes we have committed to distance.

In Ralph Ellison's *Invisible Man* the brutality is there, but it is a brutality chastened by Freud and Frazer and Joyce and mother wit. Ellison serves up his ferocity with intense calculation, his humor with elaborate premeditations; we can take the elevator up and down the levels of irony. The blood flows in diagrams. This widely celebrated novel is dizzyingly ingenious and, by any standard, major. Its shortcomings are inextricable from its marvelous inventiveness, for there is finally something pat and self-congratulatory about many key sequences and symbols. A conceptual thinness and allegorical simplification is covered over by the energetic abandon of Ellison's wit. Tracing the endlessly proliferating symbology, we can scurry through the book, as one critic has done, picking off the characters with parentheses: Mr. Norton (Northern), Supercargo (Superego), Ras (Race), Tod (Death). Our blindness in racial perplexities is neat—see the blind commencement orator at a Southern Negro college and the Communists keeping a (glass) eye out for the Negro problem.

With seemingly endless versatility Mr. Ellison has committed the racial nightmare of America to such conscious and intricate rhetorical treatment that the straight, unadorned prose of Richard Wright can now seem to us primitive. And Wright did not sufficiently trust his own sharp perceptions. Richard Gilman has concluded that Wright was "simply not a good writer, not even a competent one" because he was "so liable to lapses of taste, so unsubtly enamored of literary effects." Wright's mannerisms and his recherché epigraphs are gestures; a self-educated man, he tries desperately to prove himself really "literary" to the cultural establishment. And he usually has his eye on the boys in the back room, eager to insert a few pages of political wisdom. Self-education was not his only problem in this regard; he endured for a decade a violently defective "enlightenment" at the hands of the Communist Party. In most of his work Richard Wright is caught in double duty: he tries to find his way as artist through his way as militant spokesman. The failure in the third section of *Native Son* is the failure at the center of so much literary art of the 1930's in this country, a confusion of the obligations of art with the function of propaganda. James Baldwin has written of his exasperation when arguing in the Paris cafés with his "spiritual father"; when Wright cried that all literature was protest, Baldwin "could only weakly counter that all literature might be protest, but all protest was not literature."

Wright's errors and deficiencies are large. To ignore the radical insecurity of his talent is a serious mistake, a mistake that too many early reviewers made as they fell all over themselves to welcome a real live black man into the house of books. Yet, if we look at one of his lesser works, *12 Million Black Voices: A Folk History of the Negro in the United States,* we can begin to see the reasons for the violence and uncertainty of his writing. *12 Million Black Voices* is a picture book; Wright's text is a running caption. The photographs snap us back onto the empirical terrain of the rhetoric and the frantic need Wright felt for it. There is a photo of a depleted, hunched man standing with a dazed grin in a barren dirt yard with his shanty behind him and his gnomelike little wife and their fourteen children standing around, some with backs to the camera, some off to the right, the family like a crowd after the violence has passed. All framed by a tree barren of leaves and a fence more down than up. The prose begins to make sense; we turn a page and there, in our hands, the body of a mustached barefoot half-naked black man, his blood spattered all over

him, great holes dug out in his arms, and ten white men
rubbernecking at the camera with crazed moronic eyes, hats
on, dragging little cigarettes.

Richard Wright did not see those men from afar. He met
them head on. The chilling thing about the relationship
between the Robert Nixon case and *Native Son* is that the
novel is not "based on" the actual event. Wright was half-
through the first draft of his book before the crime occurred.
And where life imitates art with such grotesque accuracy,
the art of Richard Wright is not really an "interpretation"
of the Negro problem in America. His best work—in the
first two sections of *Native Son*, in a handful of short stories,
and in an American classic, *Black Boy*—is the literature of
survival.

I I

Yet this line will not entirely do, for it does not adequately
connect us. To argue that for most of Richard Wright's work
one must remember it before encountering it, must see it
in its historical place and gather those tensions and climates
of ignorance, is a way of accounting for his stridency, for
the broadness of his stroke. We can see Wright clearly as
a man of his time. We do not see how he is also a man of
ours. History may indeed justify certain attitudes, prejudices, failings; and a work of art should be seen in its context. But all that we know, and if it is enough for literary
historians or for professional students of cultural change,
it does not come to adequate terms with the question of
what permanent insights Richard Wright achieved. It only
makes him more definitely a "historical and sociological
document."

An argument between Irving Howe and Ralph Ellison
over Wright (most of which Howe includes in *A World*

More Attractive and Ellison in *Shadow and Act*) directs the
question. In his essay on "Black Boys and Native Sons," Mr.
Howe makes large claims:

> The day *Native Son* appeared, American culture was changed
> forever. No matter how much qualifying the book might later
> need, it made impossible a repetition of the old lies. In all its
> crudeness, melodrama and claustrophobia of vision, Richard
> Wright's novel brought out into the open, as no one ever had
> before, the hatred, fear and violence that have crippled and may
> yet destroy our culture.

Wright broke down the wall, and white America could
see something that it had not previously been able to perceive. But how clearly did Wright himself see what he was
doing? Mr. Howe answers the question with care and intelligence:

> The distinction between objective rendering and subjective im-
> mersion becomes still more difficult, perhaps even impossible.
> For a novelist who has lived through the searing experiences
> that Wright has there cannot be much possibility of approach-
> ing his subject with the "mature" poise recommended by high-
> minded critics. What is more, the very act of writing his novel,
> the effort to confront what Bigger Thomas means to him, is
> for such a writer a way of dredging up and then perhaps shed-
> ding the violence that society has pounded into him. Is Bigger
> an authentic projection of social reality, or is he a symptom of
> Wright's "dependence on violence and shock"? Obviously both;
> and it could not be otherwise.

All of which is quite to the difficult point. But Howe did not
realize just what kind of a cat he was letting out of the bag,
or, to use Mr. Ellison's terms, just what kind of cat he was
putting into the "jug." Ellison responded that "evidently
Howe feels that unrelieved suffering is the only 'real' Negro
experience, and that the true Negro writer must be
ferocious." Ellison said no white Jew was going to tell him
"it could not be otherwise":

One unfamiliar with what Howe stands for would get the impression that when he looks at a Negro he sees not a human being but an abstract embodiment of living hell. To deny in the interest of revolutionary posture that such possibilities of human richness exist for others, even in Mississippi, is not only to deny us our humanity but to betray the critic's commitment to social reality. Critics who do so should abandon literature for politics.

What has happened here is pretty clear; Ellison is a tough cat who has just been sprayed with water; he rears up hissing. At Wright as much as at Howe. When *Native Son* appeared, the reviewer for the New York *Times,* Peter Munro Jack, said that "Mr. Wright does spoil his story at the end by insisting on Bigger's fate as representative of the whole Negro race. . . ." Bigger's lawyer, Boris Max, cries out in the courtroom, "Multiply Bigger Thomas twelve million times, allowing for environmental and temperamental variations . . . and you have the psychology of the Negro people." Wright could title one of his little Leftist poems "Ah Feels It in Mah Bones"; but when Ellison sees the feelings of Bigger Thomas he cries out, "I don't feel *that* in *my* bones."

To a certain degree one can sympathize with Mr. Ellison; he is, after all, from the ventilated plains of Oklahoma, not from the Deep South, and he is offended when a black man from Natchez, or a white one from New York, defines "the Negro people" as violence and suffering, and then by implication (to get closer to the real center of the argument) chastizes the black man as artist for relaxing the reins of militancy. Ellison will not go along—not with "ferocity" and not with the major premise of Wright's work; Ellison complains that "Wright believed in the much abused idea that novels are 'weapons'—the counterpart of the dreary notion, common among most minority groups, that novels are instruments of good public relations." Ellison makes his own sense, and one must grant him his choice (refusal) of weapons—although when, in his remarks, he rages that he fears Howe's cultural dictation more than he fears the racists in the South, he has clearly lost control. Mr. Ellison deserves the reward of his own definitions, resolutely insisting that "it is not skin color which makes a Negro American. . . ."

The two positions taken here in the intense polemics of Ellison and Howe appear in constant conflict in James Baldwin's famous essay, "Many Thousands Gone." Baldwin is not able to resolve the contradiction, but he does realize the impossibility of avoiding self-contradiction on the problem that is itself so endlessly contradictory. He grants that *Native Son* is "the most powerful and celebrated statement we have yet had of what it means to be a Negro in America," but he objects that Wright did not adequately present the Negroes who surround Bigger, "his hard-working mother, his ambitious sister, his poolroom cronies, Bessie," all of whom "might be considered as far richer and far more subtle and accurate illustrations of the ways in which Negroes are controlled in our society and the complex techniques they have evolved for their survival." In Wright's book, part of the power is a false power and Baldwin concludes that *"Native Son* does not convey the altogether savage paradox of the American Negro's situation."

Yet elsewhere in his essay, and on other occasions in print and in public speech, Baldwin indicates a certain uneasiness with his attack. He senses that somehow he was measuring Wright's book by the wrong yardstick, asking it to do what it never set out to do. *Native Son,* perhaps, was up to something else. Baldwin goes on in his essay to make an extraordinary claim: "No American Negro exists who does not have his private Bigger Thomas living in the skull." And ten years later he would rephrase the same message at a symposium on "The Negro in American Culture" when he declared that "to be a Negro in this country and to be relatively conscious, is to be in a rage almost all the time." Perhaps the thing of crucial importance about Bigger Thomas was that "to tell his story is to begin to liberate us from his image."

The "savage paradox," the infinitely complex adjustments of the black community, Wright was later to try to set forth in fictional terms. In his adopted country, France, he wrote *The Long Dream*, a study of the ties that bind white to black in the South. It is a book bristling with all the intricacies of consciousness and act, all the little and large compromises, the vast network of associations that the black man in a Southern town has with the white. The book is of considerable interest and it is obviously created out of Wright's taking to heart the judgments of Ellison and Baldwin and others against *Native Son*. Yet *The Long Dream* is not nearly so important a book as *Native Son*, and seems more a story Wright was told to tell than the story he had to tell. Wright's importance lies elsewhere, lies in that ground that Ellison and Howe fought over, the ground that Baldwin keeps circling and trying to make sense of.

Wright would say, shortly before leaving for Paris, that in America he had never been able to walk two blocks without being made to feel *Negro*. As boy and as bellboy he had suffered humiliation after humiliation, beating after beating; but he was to find that even when he became a Book-of-the-Month Club man, he had not escaped. With all his money and fame, he was unable to buy a house in Vermont; and as friends of his have reported, he always tensed up when entering any new restaurant. In *12 Million Black Voices* he said that he would concern himself not with "the talented tenth" who had lifted themselves "like single fishes that leap and flash for a split second above the surface of the sea" for they were "but fleeting exceptions to that vast, tragic school that swims below in the depths, against the current, silently and heavily. . . ." But he knew that even those "fleeting exceptions" that shimmer, flashing in air, must drop sooner or later into their own environment, back into the great dragging current where their home is. Years later when he returned on a visit to America he could not see how anything had really changed. The desk clerk still lied to him at the hotel; and, in spite of all the new light being cast on the Negro problem, was not Chicago's South Side still full of Biggers? The gifted were still in pain, the mass still ruined.

In a brief statement he prepared for *Preuves* in 1958, he found a title that could be used to describe the idea in the central power of his work: *"Le Noir est une création du Blanc."* The corollary is, as Wright said in *White Man, Listen!*, "The Negro is America's metaphor." Made by whites, he himself becomes not only a figure of speech but also the explanatory image of those who named him. If Baldwin is right in claiming that no Negro exists who does not have a Bigger Thomas in his skull, something else is true, as the fantastic sales of *Native Son* indicate: the white man in America cannot escape the Bigger Thomas in *his* skull, his image of black terror that he has created. That "psychic Negro" does not just strike back and he does not just murder. He rapes. The fantasy is born of guilt. In *Native Son* the prosecuting attorney makes that quite clear, advising the court, "He killed her because he *raped* her! Mind you, Your Honor, the central crime here is *rape!*" It was not, actually.

But it was. It was in the same sense that Bigger is the Negro in America: the dirty black nigger in the national mind, an immensely cruel stupidity passed back and forth across the color line; it becomes the reality to live with, to break, to be broken by. What Baldwin is trying to illuminate in his remark about Bigger's existence in the skull is that to be black in the United States is to live with that fantasy, and all its gross and subtle consequences, as a central fact of life. Sooner or later and often, wherever a black man lives in this country, he is going to get it. There is no way to escape it, not by money, not by education, not by class. The thing won't die: not in white skull, not in black. Today a Negro Ph.D. has the door open for him at IBM (I speak of a friend) but since he is not allowed in the wealthy suburb near "the center" he has to commute (the white professional rides the train into the city, the black rides it out), and after he has gone out on the town his wife shivers in a doorway while he stands in the snow at curbside, midnight on Broadway, and watches cab after empty cab scoot by him. Helpless, he feels his Bigger coming up, crashing through degrees in solid state physics, claiming the territory.

On his first trip outside America—a brief visit to Mexico in 1940, where he met Steinbeck—Wright returned to America by train. He was in the South again and in the past, home after two decades. In the Jim Crow coach a conductor presented himself and asked about the typewriter beside Wright on the seat. The white man couldn't believe Wright's claim that he was a writer. Surely this black boy had it wrong. The conductor searched for another vocation. Now, you're a teacher? Or a preacher? You just can't be a writer. And as they talked Wright suddenly discovered "we were struggling with each other over the possession of reality."

Wright understood that struggle and what its terms were. In his folk history he said that American black people were "children of a devilish aberration, descendants of an interval of nightmare in history. . . ." Children, that is, of the beast in the American skull.

We have greatly changed, we have not changed: the

residual terror and distrust that infect all black/white relationships in this country threaten at every moment to quit
being residual. They can leap and cut with a Gem blade,
soil, and leave blocks of weeping and the dull repetitive
sameness of bottled hate in the ashes. All the old lies keep
gnawing like cracked, yellow store teeth at our sense of
what must be done and how in prudent sense it may be
legitimately, largely accomplished. Our reflexes and our
humanities are sharpened, deepened, and made subtle, but
on any street corner on any night Native Son may rise in
fire out of his ashes and here we are again, the flaming black
ghettos filling up our TV screens like summer reruns.

What was Bigger Thomas saying as he struggled to put
white womanhood into the furnace under the white mansion
if not Burn, Baby, Burn? He had no program, only instincts.
His violence was blind and private and born of a lonely,
helpless fear. It wasn't going anywhere. But just as poor,
destroyed Robert Nixon of Chicago—a movie extra in *Slave
Ship* and *Souls at Sea*—was reported by the *Tribune* as
having scrawled "Black Legion" in lipstick on Mrs. Johnson's mirror, so Bigger Thomas had in the caves of his mind
his image of "a black army."

Richard Wright was writing on a wall. His urgency does
not come from scaling that wall, nor does it come from any
capacity to show, as Ellison and Baldwin have been able to
do, how various members of the community sit on the wall
and how the Negro community as a whole has lived with it
in history, burrowing passageways for daily advance and retreat. Wright's strength and his permanent insight come
from staring at the wall itself—from various perspectives,
roaming close, touching it, butting his head against it,
measuring it—until by the very intentness and dogged determination of his single vision he sees, shows us the wall on
fire; it spurts into incandescence and begins to burn with
all the heat of this nation's monstrous capability.

CHAPTER 2

The Project

Although *Lawd Today* was not published until 1963, three years after Wright's death, it was his first book. Begun in the mid-thirties and finished in 1937, before *Uncle Tom's Children* was completed, *Lawd Today* is a day in the life of Jake Jackson, a Chicago Negro who works in the post office and hates just about everything.

The day on which all the action occurs is February 12, Lincoln's birthday. That irony is prefabricated; its presence throughout the narrative—no one can turn on the radio without getting words on the Great Emancipator—is obtrusive. Wright has to step in every few pages to point his finger at the calendar, unwilling to let Jake's winter day speak for itself. And when he does try to let that day speak, Wright is unsure of its emphasis; there are long, tedious stretches of dialogue and detail that seem less like fiction and more like sections of a tape recorder which Wright turned on and forgot to turn off:

> "How you today, Bob?"
> "Soso. How's yourself?"
> "Aw, pretty good. What you know?"
> "Nothing. Same old 6's and 7's. What you know?"
> "Nothing, man. I was just passing and thought I'd drop in."
> "I'm glad you come. I was just setting here wishing somebody'd come along."
> "If Al and Slim'd come over we could have a good game of bridge."
> "Yeah, Lawd. Set down."
> "O.K."
> "Smoke?"
> "Naw, got some."
> They lit cigarettes and puffed awhile silently.
> "How's the weather out?"
> "Swell. Feels like spring."
> "I sure wish summer'd hurry up and come on."
> "Yeah, give me summer any day."
> "Me too, boy."
> "But we got a lot of cold weather coming yet."
> "Oh, no doubt of that."
> "March'll bring a lot of cold blizzards."
> "And April a lot of sleet and rain."
> "Yeah, we got a lot of cold weather coming yet."
> "Oh, yeah."

And so *on*. Some of it is funny, really funny—especially if one tries to read it aloud and discovers that it begins to sound like Ionesco—and Wright's point here is surely the pointlessness. Yet he works this device too often, trying to convey the helpless jawing the men go through to fill up the void (which only makes the void seem larger). Wright overestimates our tolerance, our capacity to keep reading blanks. It is a major flaw of the book: the card games are interminable, the post office section goes on much too long; randomness, everything stretched; it is not really a novel. *Lawd Today* is a long story unwound.

But it has impressive moments. One interesting feature in the context of Wright's other work is that the sex in *Lawd Today* is not the sex that Wright usually creates. That is, the sex here is not stagey, not "written"; it is simply there, in the characters. In *Lawd Today* sexual brutality hangs everywhere—in the waitress, in the pornographic post cards, in the dive—and Wright does not make a fuss about it, does not overwrite it; in later things he would either dress it up (in "Long Black Song," for example, "her blood surged like the long gladness of summer") or suddenly insert it, staging little dull erotic intervals that have nothing to do with the characters. The sex in Jake Jackson's story is never self-consciously pretty; it is a legitimate dimension of Jake's personality and a legitimate part of his story's importance.

In that story we are shown the cumulative effects of organized brutality and repression. An outcome of that brutality and repression is recorded in catalogs of the grossest (and the funniest) piles of odd lore, sexual misinformation, and general spiritual quackery. The numbers game does not involve just desperate chances, a frantic gamble; it also involves magic clairvoyants who, by reading your dreams, can tell you the right number to play. "THE MYSTERIOUS THREESTAR MEDIUM" proclaims "LADIES AND GENTLEMEN: LEND ME YOUR EARS!! I MAKE NUMBERS COME OUT IN ASHES." We thumb the *King Solomon's Wheel of Life and Death Dream Book* and check out the "Bossmanrow." This reliance on magic appears even in the elaborate, formal insults, The Dozens, which has a chanting undertone of incantation and spell. It is a world of magic cure-alls, snake charmers, mysterious folk traditions of obscenity, Old-Time Religion carnival shows and "DOCTOR WILLIAM LOUIS SPEEDY'S POWERFUL IMPOTENCY CASTIGATOR."

The point of all this is a clear and important one. In *Black Boy* Wright has a catalog of boyhood superstitions; he concludes that since "I had no power to make things happen outside of me in the objective world, I made things happen within. Because my environment was bare and bleak, I endowed it with unlimited potentialities, redeemed it for the sake of my own hungry and cloudy yearning." And the spells and superstitions persist with an equally important role on into manhood, performing new and more complicated tasks. Frantz Fanon writes in *The Wretched of the Earth* that

the native will strengthen the inhibitions which contain his aggressiveness by drawing on the terrifying myths which are so frequently found in underdeveloped countries. There are maleficent spirits which intervene every time a step is taken in the wrong direction, leopard-men, serpent-men, six-legged dogs, zombies . . . the occult sphere is a sphere belonging to the community which is entirely under magical jurisdiction. By entangling myself in this inextricable network where actions are repeated with crystalline inevitability, I find the everlasting world which belongs to me, and the perenniality which is thereby affirmed of the world belonging to us.

Jake Jackson falls prey, all the bad day long, to the most elemental ignorances dressed up as supernatural magic powers. He is unable to get at his real enemy, the white man with his elaborate technology, the huge efficient system which has put the black man under a spell—unable to get at it except to be one of the little pieces of that system, a pair of black hands shuffling through mail in the caverns of the post office. Jake tries to live and figure out all his dirty little crises, get rich, get rid of his wife's *"Gawddamn tumor"* by throwing himself on the mercy of the Gods of Numerology and by sending away to "THE SUREFIRE TREATMENT COMPANY, INC."

The book is a side show. It is a hopeless, helpless carnival of brutalization: the whites to blacks, the blacks to blacks, circles of violence that spin like a Squirrel Cage (as the mid-section of the book is called), where you can't get out and can only endure the terror of minute-by-minute brutality until an act of special brutality puts you out of commission, in jail or cut up on the street. This vision of hell is done, however, without moaning and without pious requests for our tears; the energy and the comic invention keep blaring like the lights and music at a side show. The costumes are splendid:

Because he was wearing the green suit, he decided on low-cut, brown suede shoes with high Cuban heels and toes that tapered to a point. He tied the shoestrings in a neat, tight bow. Spotlessly white spats capped the bargain. Next, he put on a soft-collared lavender shirt which contrasted pleasingly with his broad, red elastic suspenders. Then he tried a black tie, a green tie, a brown tie, and a red tie. In the end he selected a wide yellow one studded with tiny blue halfmoons. He added a delicate finish-ing touch by inserting a huge imitation ruby that burned like a smear of fresh blood. Squaring his shoulders, he buttoned coat and vest and adjusted with sensitive fingers the purple em-broidered orange handkerchief that peeped out of his breast pocket. He sprayed each of his coat lapels with violet-scented perfume, then pivoted on his heels in the middle of the rug and brought himself to a sudden halt in front of the dresser mirror. "Like a Maltese kitten," he said.

All dressed up, and no place to go. Nowhere, that is, except the jazzier corners of the cage. Jake Jackson bears many re-semblances to Bigger Thomas and he is clearly a first try at creating the Native Son. Like Bigger, Jake is a black rat caught in the Chicago trap. Yet the trap in *Lawd Today* is not the sudden vice grip of *Native Son*; it is, instead, the squirrel cage of numbing and extravagantly bright repeti-tions. At the end of the book, drunk and rolled, Jake goes back to the wife who has fallen asleep on her knees, praying at the bedside, the "bitch with the tumor." As Jake stumbles home, bleeding and broke, with only eighty-five cents left of his loan of a hundred dollars, he smiles. He yells, "BUT WHEN I WAS FLYING I WAS A FLYING FOOL!" And the movie marquee he had seen earlier in the day now floats up in his mind—the aviator of the silver screen, the flying fool of white America. A car lashes by and Jake can only think, as he crisscrosses, *Got to be careful. Can't get run over.*

But he has been.

This worthy start in *Lawd Today* would have to appear only as a posthumous record; Wright's real breakthrough into recognition was *Uncle Tom's Children*. The book won the five-hundred-dollar Federal Writers' Projects prize offered by *Story* magazine. Out of the hundreds of submissions, the judges (Sinclair Lewis was one) said that Wright's collection of novellas was the obvious choice, by far the most powerful piece of writing that had come to them. When the book was published, the reviewers were almost unanimous in their praise.

The book as it is reprinted today is not quite the book that won the prize. *Uncle Tom's Children* was expanded in 1940, after the great success of *Native Son*, to include Wright's essay "The Ethics of Living Jim Crow," which had first appeared in *American Stuff*, an anthology of work done on the Federal Writers' Project, and his story "Bright and Morning Star" originally published in *New Masses* in 1939. These additions distort the over-all design of the book and need not be considered at any great length here; almost everything valuable in "The Ethics of Living Jim Crow" would find its way a half-dozen years later into *Black Boy*, and "Bright and Morning Star" does little more than reiterate the lesson of the final story in the original *Uncle Tom's Children,* "Fire and Cloud," showing how the central figure moves from abject Christian faith to militance. And "Bright and Morning Star" shines with Wright's worst rhetoric: "She stood up and looked at the floor while call and counter-call, loyalty and counter-loyalty struggled in her soul. Mired she was between two abandoned worlds. . . ." The story makes no new case, only repeats one. When Wright would retell the incident on which "Bright and Morning Star" was based, in *Black Boy,* his prose would be more adequate to its terrifying pain.

As one critic, Eleanor Roosevelt, has written, *Uncle Tom's Children* is a book about "the tragedy of fear." In its title as in other things, it looks back to *Uncle Tom's Cabin* and to that lady writer who knew very well the power of the Gothic and how to use that tradition's clichés for her propaganda pictures of horror. Mrs. Stowe's book is able to convey, even to a reader today, considerable force; the tract accumulates that force by use of a deep religious overcurrent and the stereotypes of nineteenth-century sentimentalism. In Uncle Tom's journey southward to suffering and death there is a kind of masochistic ecstasy, sacrificial bliss; all the power of the second half of the novel is Uncle Tom, the Black Christ. He gives his life for the many. After the brutal whipping he reads, "the life of Him by whose stripes we are healed." And with his death comes the vision of Christ.

In calling his book *Uncle Tom's Children,* Wright refers us to this mythic father, makes his characters the progeny of a stereotype and brings his book into the family of protest literature. These "children" are different. They refuse to be like their father, an object of pity. This is "another generation which says—'Uncle Tom is dead!' " Wright's first try at the novel was focused on the urban life of the migrants to the North; here in the long stories he goes back, in history and in his own life, to the South. We go "down home," where the question of life is simple: how to survive. These are stories of extraordinary and unrelieved violence; if the Negro is America's metaphor, this piece of the system has all the weight of the culture's violence behind it. The violence comes with such unrelenting directness, in such unbroken and unrelieved totality, that the community becomes nothing more, or less, than organized insanity.

In the writing of the first story, "Big Boy Leaves Home," Wright was pushed beyond what seems to have been its original function as the first in a coherent lesson plan leading to the final declaration of strength. The ways in which "Big Boy Leaves Home" breaks out of its position as What Happens When You Aren't Strong are sufficiently complex to put it aside momentarily until we can see the general design of the book.

In each of the four stories Wright broadens the areas of responsibility on the part of each succeeding main character, moving from boy to community leader, from victim to victor, so that the stories will compose a rising tide of militancy. When the book ends with the cry of black triumph, *"Freedom belongs t the strong,"* we are to see it not just as the end of that story but as the point toward which all the stories have been moving.

However effective such a motion may be in terms of practical encouragement, it does not entirely work. The first story, a study of pain and loss and brutal defeat, is the finest thing in the book and one of the finest things Wright ever did; the final story, showing the Reverend Dan Taylor's development from old handkerchief-head parson to militant leading the army clearly is intended as an object lesson, but its final scene of triumph is far less convincing than its central character.

Like his next and most famous work, *Native Son, Uncle*

Tom's Children provides a challenging premise in its open-ing image of racial nightmare ("Big Boy Leaves Home") and then leaves us with the Party-line "message" of the con-clusion ("Fire and Cloud"). The two middle stories of the collection, "Down by the Riverside" and "Long Black Song," are of only secondary interest—the first marred by serious plotting difficulties and the second by passages of purple prose. The stories have, however, a functional im-portance for the book as a whole, each one lifting us up a step from victimization to self-assertion. In the floodwaters of "Down by the Riverside" it is inevitable that sooner or later Brother Mann will kill—as inevitable as the fact that sooner or later he will be killed. But in that insane circum-stance he does exhibit remarkable capacities for endurance and brave action. Then, in "Long Black Song," we move up another step; when a band of crackers sets his house on fire Silas stays inside, achieving a ferocious brute dignity by sim-ply refusing to come out. You shall be deprived of the pleas-ure. Never see my body. Never get to mutilate it. Silas cannot win, but he can lose with terrific dignity. He had "killed as many as he could and stayed on to burn, had stayed without a murmur."

Wright despised pity. In one of his routine articles for the *Daily Worker* (August 4, 1937), he wrote of "Negro, with 3-Week-Old Baby, Begs Food on Streets." At the end of the column Wright said, "If you are the type to weep, you can have a good cry over this and then feel good, 'purged,' you know." Wright refused to let his readers off the hook and he hated to serve up suffering for moments of easy moral exercise. (And that is a major reason *Black Boy* is large, avoiding self-pity and not asking ours.) In these two middle stories of *Uncle Tom's Children,* Brother Mann and Silas are, in death, heroic. Their voices are echoed in the voice of the poor mother in the story added later, "Bright and

Morning Star," who does not just carry a winding sheet for her son but carries a gun inside it. Her cry at the end is what Silas could have cried, "Yuh didn't get what yuh wanted." These are the people who say Uncle Tom is dead; they say it by refusing to go down as he did, in sweetness and in the pathos of white light. Here is part of the reason why militants in the black movement insist on Wright's name; although his characters are victims of racism, they also assert a black pride. These are the true parents. Not an end but a beginning. From them grow all the possibilities of remedial action.

But individual acts of heroism, great personal moments, also show how futile the act of rebellion is if it is only a private matter. Brother Mann, Silas, and Johnny-Boy's magnificent old mother display extraordinary courage. They are killed for it. Their triumph is to die well. And so *Uncle Tom's Children* concludes with "Fire and Cloud," in which private courage is subsumed in collective action.

It is a story about political pressure. Early in the action, when the main character, Dan Taylor, "swallowed," he has to swallow just about everything. The leader of his people, the most powerful black man in the community, he tries to keep his position, only to discover that in order to keep it he must nicely calculate how much to take, how much to give, and finally it's a rotten deal. It will not work even though he wants to keep things on an even keel for the future, for his son's sake, the boy who will be "a leader of his people someday." As Dan says, "thas the one hope of mah life."

But, as the story shows, all the hopes of Dan Taylor's life were writ in water. It just won't go. "Ah done lived all mah life on mah knees, a-beggin n a-pleadin wid the white folks. N all they gimme wuz crumbs! All they did wuz kick me!" After the white man beat him, after they make him pray aloud to the tune of the whip, Taylor walks home through the white neighborhood "like a pillar of fire" to lead his flock down freedom road. His son, Jimmy, has been pushing Taylor to militance all through the story ("Aw, hell, Pa! Is we gonna be dogs *all* the time?"). Taylor explains to his boy the faith of the future:

> "Membah whut Ah tol yuh prayer wuz, son?"
> There was silence, then Jimmy answered slowly:
> "Yuh mean lettin Gawd be so real in yo life tha everthing yuh do is cause of Im?"
> "Yeah, but its different now, son. It's the *people!* Theys the ones whut mus be real t us!"

And Taylor finally climbs on the bandwagon that has been waiting for him; he goes out and joins the swelling tide, the great band of marchers singing of the fire by night and the cloud by day; under the waves of their song and "moving with a sea of placards and banners" they storm into the town; the mayor buckles and promises food if the folks go home. The story ends in "a baptism of clean joy" and the triumph of the new masses.

In its characters, in its plot, and in its ultimate message "Fire and Cloud" embodies the program of "Proletarian Realism" advocated by the cultural commission of the Communist Party: "The villains should be the southern planters and the Wall Street bankers. The plots should be simple and clear . . . should conclude on a note of triumph, the victory of the black proletarian over his white oppressors." In his previous stories Wright had portrayed the villains of the system; he had done it in a clear and direct way; he had described the degradations of the lower classes—all key tasks in the Party's plan for the new literature. But only with "Fire and Cloud" was the final objective reached. Mike Gold, occupant of the cultural chair for the *Daily Worker,* had formulas for Proletarian Realism. He included one very important point: the new writers should not just pick through the ash can of the present; they should write always with "the hope of the future; revolutionary *élan* will sweep this mess out of the world forever."

"Fire and Cloud" may be based, as so many of Wright's works are, on an actual incident. Angelo Herndon, a Negro, a Birmingham coal miner, was the center of a famous case in the thirties, when he was sentenced to twenty years on the chain gang for "inciting to insurrection." In an autobiographical pamphlet he described an uprising that very well could have been the model for Wright's story. In a *Daily Worker* article—"Mrs. Holmes and Daughters Drink From the Fountain of Communism"—Wright described an elderly Harlem woman who had put Herndon's picture on the wall. Mrs. Holmes is quoted by Wright as telling her daughters about Herndon's demonstration of whites and blacks united to get bread. He "told the Southern landlords that they could not kill the working class." Herndon's pamphlet speaks for itself: .

In the middle of June, 1932, the state closed down all the relief stations. A drive was organized to send all the jobless to the farms.

We gave out leaflets calling for a mass demonstration at the courthouse to demand that the relief be continued. About 1,000 workers came, 600 of them white. We told the commissioners we didn't intend to starve. We reminded them that $800,000 had been collected in the Community Chest drive. The commissioners said there wasn't a cent to be had.

But the very next day the commission voted $6,000 for relief to the jobless!

There is a reason beyond the *Daily Worker* article to think Wright got his idea from Herndon. Wright must have been somewhat troubled by the claim that whites would march shoulder to shoulder with blacks (he offers no explanation in his story and never reports in other writing having seen white and black in the South join like this). In Herndon's

account there are 1,000—600 white, 400 black, a ratio of
3:2. In Wright's story, the agitators Hadley and Greene
promise 5,000, saying they have 3,000 whites and 2,000
blacks. Again, exactly 3:2, white to black, as in Herndon's
account. Since Wright was unable to offer evidence of how
the racial unity was achieved, it is understandable that he
should want to stick closely (and in what little detail he
had) to an actual account.

"Fire and Cloud" is about Dan Taylor. The story's considerable power pulls us directly to the center of Taylor's
agonizing struggle, and we encounter everything through
Taylor's eyes. We are immersed in the black leader's
dilemma and viscerally attacked by his humiliations and
physical torture. The story convincingly portrays his conversion. Wright knows the Dan Taylors, knows the tensions
and pressures that move those men. Taylor is a man of
sagacity, and he has been able to work well in the past to get
some things accomplished for his people. He hates the racist
game, but he has decided that it's better to play it, and play
it as well as he can, because if he does not he does nothing.
His encounter with the mayor is a paradigm of his whole
life; the mayor wants to use him: "It'll take a lot more than
a summer cold to kill old war-horses like you and me, eh,
Dan?" But in time of famine the white community has to
hold on to the crumbs that they had previously handed to
Dan; he sees that he can no longer go "a-begging." He is
forced to see it in a scene of incredible torture and humiliation when the white thugs tie him to a tree. As they whip
him, "warm blood" seeping "down into his trousers," they
make him pray. It is a brutal parody of all that he is—the
pious pastor under the white lash—and suddenly his role in
the black community and his faith become inseparable from
whipping. Sobbing "Hallowed be Thy name" as the whip
cuts into him, he cracks. But to crack is to be saved. He

achieves a writhing dignity as he cries out, "Awright, kill me! Tie me n kill me! Yuh white trash cowards, kill me!" But they don't; the mayor still thinks that when Dan is softened up he will come along.

He will not, for the brutality has opened him to the life of his community: "Ah know whut yo life is! Ah done felt it! Its *fire!* Its like the fire that burned me las night! Its sufferin! Its hell! Ah cant bear this fire erlone!" He can bear it with them. Hovering between black world and white he had a certain small effectiveness; forced now to find his only true home in the black world, his effectiveness is considerably enlarged.

Or is it? When *Uncle Tom's Children* was published, Granville Hicks's review in the *New Masses* was full of praise, but he had a small objection: "Apparently Wright is so eager to move ahead with the main action that he will not pay sufficient attention to subordinate details even when they are essential." And these subordinate details are essential to the final scene of the story where the cry of triumph rings. We are in a small Southern city of 25,000. Hadley, one of the agitators, predicts that if Taylor will stop holding out and give his endorsement, they will be able to deliver "five thousand easily" at the march. Hadley and his sole companion, Greene, are surely two of the most fantastically efficient organizers who ever lived, even in proletarian fiction. Without the approval of the spiritual leader of the community, these two have been able to get in and energize that community of thousands, so that they will follow if Dan leads. Hadley and Greene can promise that the town will be covered with handbills on a twelve-hour notice and they can deliver "a sea of placards and banners" for the big day.

Dan Taylor's dilemma is not really to arouse his people, but whether or not to join them. Yet, if we look back at the

other black communities in *Uncle Tom's Children*—those of
"Big Boy Leaves Home" and "Down by the Riverside" (there
is no sense of community in "Long Black Song," only a
single shack)—we see that they face their crises only in total
submission. They have no political thoughts; they go down
in abject terror and helplessness. One is swamped by water,
the other razed by fire. Nothing can be done. If the community in "Fire and Cloud" is a lesson in difference, where
was that lesson learned? It could be argued that the situation in "Fire and Cloud" is overpoweringly desperate:
Brother Bonds brings reports of mass beatings, women and
children, the killing of one black man "whut tried t fight
back," and white vigilantes "ridin up n down in cars." Yet
this parade of horrors is a direct result of the threat to
march and not a cause of it. The determination of the community to get to City Hall occasions the first battles of race
war, not the other way around.

And would the poor whites join the poor blacks? When
in the spring of 1932 the *Crisis* solicited opinion from
prominent Negro newspaper editors about Communism,
Frank M. Davis of Georgia's *Atlanta World* responded:

The Negro as a whole fears Communism—probably because white
America has not accepted it. Some frankly believe Red promises
would be forgotten were they in power, for aren't they white
men too? Further: would the average, every-day white man be
willing to forget his prejudices . . . ?

One answer to that question came in 1957 in Macon County,
Alabama. The Tuskegee Civic Association held a selective-
buying campaign directed against white merchants. Stokely
Carmichael and Charles V. Hamilton point out in their
book, *Black Power* (pp. 133–4), that the TCA-led boycott
"lasted for about four years at a high level of effectiveness.
During a period of two years, twenty-six businesses operated
by whites closed down. But even then, the whites did not

give in. . . . Apparently, the whites were willing to suffer economic disaster rather than concede political power to the blacks."

The lessons of Southern history and the lessons of Richard Wright's own previous work negate the lesson of "Fire and Cloud." At the end we are told that the demonstrators

sang as they marched. More joined along the way. When they reached the park that separated the white district from the black, the poor whites were waiting. Taylor trembled when he saw them join, swelling the mass that moved toward the town. He looked ahead and saw black and white marching; he looked behind and saw black and white marching. And still they sang. . . .

And we must "tremble" too, with Taylor, at the sudden appearance of these mobilized crackers. In the entire book of *Uncle Tom's Children* there is only a single portrait of an unprejudiced white—Hadley, the Northern Communist. In "Fire and Cloud" thousands of whites—the poorest, traditionally the greatest haters of the Negro—decide to join with their economic brothers for bread. In *Uncle Tom's Children* the central passion of every Southern white man is black hatred. Faced with the choice of uniting with Negro or dying by famine, the redneck of *Uncle Tom's Children* would die. What actually is going on in those marching ranks at the end of the story? Here people are marching for what seems to be the first time in their lives, marching in vast numbers where black and white are meeting as partners. How are they looking at each other in this sudden and revolutionary alliance; is there any physical contact, do these Southern whites and blacks really march arm in arm? Wright passes, and concludes in a swab of rhetoric where every practical question is solved by figures of speech. All the prose on the last two pages is bloated, throbbing with triumph at the expense of accuracy. Even Dan Taylor himself ceases to be an interesting figure and becomes a stock emblem of the good leader as "he felt neither fear nor joy, just an humble confidence in himself. . . ." *An* humble confidence? His eyes grow "wet with tears."

The problem is that while Wright got Dan Taylor and Dan Taylor's agony from his own background as a Southern black man, to end the story—and the book—Wright got his "revolutionary *élan*" from a pamphlet and the optimism of his comrades. In "Fire and Cloud" we know Dan Taylor, Wright makes us know him; the forces that give his conversion a social triumph do not exist. At the end he is joined to something extra. On the final pages we must accept a *deus* (*Marxus*) *ex machina*. If Dan had gone out to lead his black congregation, and the police shot him to death (three hundred of them with no evidence that they would exercise restraint) how would the story change? It would make Dan another Brother Mann, another Silas—or, that is, his heroism at the top of the ladder would be a complement of theirs at the bottom. Wright could not bear to say that, for it would end the book with hopelessness: even the best are doomed to fall. But he could not provide the evidence for us to believe the opposite, to gather a firm ground for the march to freedom. We remain impressed by Taylor's dilemma, not its resolution. Wright felt Taylor's dilemma, knew how to make it live in the southland; the resolution he had heard about and wanted desperately to believe in. All through *Uncle Tom's Children* Wright had been digging deeply into the black pit of the racial nightmare and he had dug so deeply that at the end he looks up and is paralyzed by a suspicion that escape is impossible. So he hops out. And stands singing the "International." Wright's greatest gift was his knowledge of where the darker recesses of the cave were and how to get to them. One of his greatest achievements, as a writer and as a man, was his unkillable determination to go on digging. It is not surprising, then, that the real triumph of his first book would not be at the end, where he tries to lift himself out of the South with the aid of the Party, but at the beginning, where he would go in on his own, armed only with his native tools, to expose the vast caverns of the wound.

"Big Boy Leaves Home" stands in the very front rank of Wright's work; the story first appeared in the *New Caravan* (November 2, 1936), and he would never in the next two decades of published writing achieve a greater success in the story form. One critic has said that " 'Big Boy Leaves Home' shows that crime inevitably springs from the denial of adequate recreational facilities." It goes a bit farther than that.

Wright would object, later, that what bothered him about *Uncle Tom's Children* is that it made too many bankers' daughters cry. And on the surface "Big Boy Leaves Home" should be the one story in the book that would appear most guilty of that charge; Big Boy does not even have the saving grace of a Silas, a dignity in death, or the revolutionary conversion of a Dan Taylor. Big Boy just runs. He is a poor victim of unbearable brutality and he is a victim only. A helpless boy. Yet the story does not really invoke tears or it invokes them secondarily from those unwilling to take its full import. The real object of "Big Boy" is terror, and it presents that terror as inseparable from a deep and pervasive myth, fraught with sexual pathology. The writing is clear, cleansed of any phoniness or sloganeering, perfectly in control.

"Big Boy Leaves Home" sets the pitch for *Uncle Tom's Children* as a whole. It strikes the major chord, establishes the energies and symbols and directions that will be elaborated in all the subsequent stories. The great pond at the beginning and the torrential rains will appear again in the flood in "Down by the Riverside." The sexual encounter between white and black recurs in "Long Black Song." And the burning of the black boy, Bobo, is an explosion of flame that will burst up again both on Silas's shack and on the "pillar of fire" that Dan Taylor feels walking home. Big Boy's dream of the newspaper headlines, "NIGGER KILLS DOZEN OF MOB BEFO LYNCHED" and "TRAPPED NIGGER SLAYS TWENTY BEFO KILLED," prefigure Silas's last stand. In all these, and in its general theme of race hate and massive violence, "Big Boy" is an introduction.

Yet none of the subsequent stories is able to come up to "Big Boy Leaves Home." It is a definitive statement, a great story; it locates and embodies the blood pools of history in one incident of racial trouble. And it is utter horror understood.

We hear the boys before we see them. The sexual image, the importance in the plot of clothes, the bantering insult and the humor, all these are in that first line: *"YO MAMA don wear no drawers. . . ."* It is as if the trees have begun to talk; the voice "rose out of the woods" and the melodious lines of insult and folk humor float for eight lines, in scenery, before the characters step onto the stage. Four black boys walk "lollingly in bare feet, beating tangled vines and bushes with long sticks" as if to flush out game (as later the whites will roam, beating, trying to flush out their human game). All here at the outset is sweet and easy: the ground is warm "Jus lika bed" and, "Ah kin feel tha ol sun goin all thu me." They keep singing, manufacturing nonsense—"a *qualls* a *quall*"—uninhibited, farting ("NIGGER, YUH BROKE WIN!"). Nature approves this play in paradise: "A black winged butterfly hovered at the water's edge. A bee droned. From somewhere came the sweet scent of honeysuckles." And in the second section of the story the boys make their way, like Tom Sawyers and Huck Finns, through the soft mythic pastures of familiar American boyhood reverie "to the swimming hole." Happy and black, they shed their clothes and frolic in the water.

The white woman appears. The boys run for their clothes; the woman screams; her companion—the Southern white man with his rifle and army officer's uniform, one of the captains and colonels that inhabit Dixie memories—comes to the rescue of white womanhood. He shoots down two of the boys, Lester and Buck, but Bobo and Big Boy overpower him and kill him. Then they run. Bobo keeps saying, as he runs, "Ahm scared"; four times he cries it out and he fears "Theys gonna lynch us." No such luck. A rope around the neck would be a blessing; beaten by Big Boy at the beginning, in the wrestling match, Bobo will be captured, mutilated, burned alive.

The boys rush home, where the parents realize what terror is waiting for them. Ma and Pa know what it's all about, for they have lived through it. It is the dread sin, the great curse—the black native naked in the presence of the white woman. And they've killed not just a white but a patriot, a "soljer." The cry goes out for the gathering of the black clan; the room is soon filled with "Brothers" and "Elders." The family keeps asking the boy why he wasn't at school, keeps putting the pointless question to him. The adult mind mumbles insanely dull patterns, over and over, as if by simply insisting on what should have been then what has been will ebb and pass away. There is nothing. The happy black boys could not get back to their clothes, cannot be civilized, cannot hide their black members. Decency was unobtainable and led to murder; after murder there is now no protection, no refuge, and the indecency grows with killing force. Big Boy has broken in on the ritual, the sexual consummation of the white world; he has killed the groom, the soldier lover of the white lady who carries her hat in her hand. And the black community sees "itll ruin us all." The murder by mistake now runs through both communities, white and black, energizing them and calling up the full consequence of the curse.

Big Boy is on his way. He has had no water since noon— but he will get it. As if anticipating that the destruction is to be by fire, Big Boy hides in the kilns, where on other "long, hot summer days" the boys had played at their dream of mobility, Casey Jones tooling down the tracks. Everywhere he turns Big Boy is in trouble. The "brown writhing mass" of a giant rattlesnake waits in the hole. All nature is after him and he thinks of a pack of dogs "foamin n howlin." From the opening paradise of country ease the brief encounter between the races at the old swimming hole has led to sheer physical terror:

When inside he felt there must be snakes about him, ready to strike. It seemed he could see and feel them there, waiting tensely in coil. In the dark he imagined long white fangs ready to sink into his neck, his side, his leg.

From afar white voices come with fire; Big Boy's family has been thrown out of their house and the house has been burned. On the opening pages we heard gentle songs of glory and happy abandoned tunes; now they are picked up by marauding bands of whites, with their own, peculiar song of glory: "We'll hang ever nigger t a sour apple tree. . . ."

They get Bobo and have a picnic. A feast: tar and feather and burn and dismember. "Look! Hes gotta finger!" "He's got one of the ears, see?" It is a community entertainment, the ladies and the gents gathered around the camp fire. Big Boy, watching from his hole, sees Bobo's body go up in flame, written against the sky; he lies there, rain begins, and he has to kill an inquisitive dog that threatens to give him away. From sunshine and honeysuckle and a summer swimming hole Big Boy has dropped out of the world into a hole filling up with cold rain, a dog's body in his lap.

In the final section Big Boy makes his escape in the back of a truck—fittingly, the "Magnolia Express Comny"—on its way to Chicago. Where Big Boy will become Bigger.

The story is put together extremely carefully; each detail Wright handles with extraordinary care. The sun, at the beginning, goes through all their bodies, warming them, smiling; after the murder "the wide glare of sun stretching out over the fields was pitiless" and at the very end, rising on a new morning, the sun is twice referred to as "blades of daylight." The land which at first is soft and warm, a bower, becomes a hole in dirt, and then at the very end gives way to the "splinters and sawdust" bouncing in the truck bed. The boys come out of the woods singing "Dis train bound fo Glory" but for them there are no trains for glory, only the fugitive truck bed (the land was "Jus lika bed"). And all of what seems to be naturalistic dialogue is part of a carefully engineered symbolic pattern, so that casual comments have a cutting edge: "Jeesus, Ah could stay here ferever" or "LAS ONE INS A OL DEAD DOG!" The opening lines refer us to later action. The wrestling match shows Big Boy's large strength—he overpowers the three of them—and shows Bobo's characteristic role, the loser, for it is his neck that Big Boy threatens to break. The last line of the first section is " 'Ahma smart nigger,' said Big Boy, thrusting out his chest." He will need to be very smart, a Big enough Boy, to escape what has been waiting for him.

Just as the little details recur—at the pool of water the white woman has her hat in her hand, at the end Big Boy drinks from a little pool of water cradled in a hat—so the central image of the story is part of one large explosion. The railroading games, where the boys work up a head of steam, letting out shrill whistles—"There were times when they had the whole hillside blazing and smoking"—are a grotesque little parody of the lynching by fire when the whites work up their head of steam. Bobo lets out a spurt of shrill high screams, and "the flames leaped tall as the trees" as the mob stands "looking up the slopes at the writhing white mass gradually growing black, growing black in a cradle of yellow flame."

When Wright's volume first appeared he was praised on all sides for his hard-nosed "realism." Here were accurate reports from a far land, reliable maps of its actual terrain. Wright was commended for the clarity of his vision, for no-nonsense accounting. No myths; the straight stuff. Yet that "realism" was rather more ambitious than the white reviewers seem to have seen. Wright's realism goes far beyond what the adolescent could see. The behavior of the white woman at the pond is observed through the terror-stricken eyes of the naked boys; there is much confusion and yelling and rifle fire. When one goes back over the story and actually traces the physical movements of the woman her steps show us something that through the hysteria of the boys we had not noticed. First, for some reason, the woman is a considerable distance away from her fiancé and it takes him some time, at least a minute, to get to her. The description of her indicates she is more than a walk-on; she has some special symbolic significance. In the atmosphere where the boys are "letting sunshine dry their skins and warm their blood," in the bower of butterfly and bee and sweet scents of honeysuckles, the woman appears "poised on the edge of the opposite embankment"—the gulf between black male and white woman—with "her hair lit by the sun." When she sees them she cries softly a single word, "Oh!" and then "the white woman backed slowly out of sight." Where does she go? The boys wait, then go for their clothes. "Twenty-five feet away the woman stood." Big Boy has good reason to be "puzzled." The woman, startled by four black boys, gets away by running to stand near their clothes. Big Boy "looked at the woman. He looked at the bundle of clothes." When Big Boy steps forward, the woman does not get out of his way; she backs even closer to the clothes until she is almost standing over them. Big Boy comes forward, "black and naked," and keeps telling her that all he wants is his clothes; the woman keeps telling him to go away, but refuses to budge from her position between their naked bodies and their clothes.

It is part of the general pattern in the story which embodies the racial confrontation in sexual terms. The behavior of the woman is composed of sexual come-on and paralyzing fear. And the Southern fantasy is itself a compound of such ambivalence; presumed Negro sexual superiority is a function of the Southern white community's own fantasies of guilt. For centuries "Massa" had been violating his black slave women; for centuries Massa's wife had been seeing mulatto children on her lawn. And the opening image of black boys swimming naked demands, for the nightmare to play itself out, to have the white woman appear, her hair lit up by the sun; the fantasy must go on to lynching, fire, the fulfillment of thwarted sexuality as violation and sadism.

The lynching is a picnic, a relief from the broad rural tedium. H. L. Mencken has written that "lynching often takes the place of the merry-go-round, the theatre, the symphony orchestra, and other diversions common to larger communities." In "Big Boy Leaves Home" it is taking the place of the sexual act itself. The women join in and they cry out in ecstasy, "Jack! Jack! Don leave me! Ah wanna see im!" Amidst cries of "sweetheart" and muttered requests for drinks,

there were women singing now. Their voices made the song round and full. Song waves rolled over the top of pine trees. The sky sagged low, heavy with clouds.

At the beginning of the story nature smiled, in light, over the free, uncontaminated sexuality of the black boys dancing naked; nature now sags low, heavy with clouds, as the white community reaches its sexual consummation. The orgasm is a burst of fire, and then the quiet afterplay of rain.

The lynching is not only vengeance, for the father is not shooting down the murderer of his son. The desire is not merely to punish—a bullet could do that—and it is not simply a public intimidation of other Negroes. No other Negro is present except Big Boy, hidden in his hole, and the retribution has already been accomplished in the burning of the black family's house. The desire, much more than a desire to punish, is a desire to enjoy. The desire is desire. In the opening dialogue of the story, four times Big Boy is called crazy—twice in capital letters—but the dominant insanity here is white. The opening was a scene of idyllic pleasure; the story, on the surface a tale of hurt and death and pain and physical discomfort and terror, is a story about pleasure. The central attainment of that pleasure comes in carving up and serving on plates of fire. The plucking off of the "SOURVINEERS," fingers and ears, becomes, symbolically, the act of ripping off the black penis; when the sacred objects are achieved—"the sky was black and the wind was blowing hard"—a woman drops down fainting—in terror? in ecstasy?—at the sight of "a tar-drenched body glistening and turning." The white community, man and woman together, achieves the release of a huge, black pain.

The mysterious motion of the white woman at the water's edge becomes clearer; or, that is, the reason for its odd vagueness becomes clear. Fear and enticement, but most importantly: entrapment. On the surface, entrapment is obviously not her motive; she goes through all the obvious gestures of utter fear; but the only reason for her walking where she does, for the symbolic associations that cluster about her and shine in her hair, all suggest that the story is turning in on itself, turning in on deeper mysteries, and refusing to accept the terms of the surface.

Wright's dialogues among whites and the little glimpses we get of the whites are often capable of at least two diametrically opposed meanings (as in the fainting of the woman at the fire), quickly said, run over. One white asks another, "Say, whuts tha yuh got?" The response is, "Er pillar." The pillow is there for feathers. Tar and all. The line is comic horror; when the word gets out that a nigger is going to be lynched, the white man runs straight to his inner room, comes up with a pillow and trots across the field with it under his arm. He's got his equipment. Got it in bed. The same grizzly comedy of sexual disgust comes across in:

> "Jack! Jack! Don leave me! Ah wanna see im!"
> "Theyre bringin im over the hill, sweetheart!"

Sweetheart. "HURRY UP N BURN THE NIGGER FO IT RAINS!" And after the consummation, as stray voices come across the field with "Wait, Charles! Don leave me; its slippery here," we hear the gentle, cavalier offer of some nameless participant in the rite: "Ahll take some of yuh ladies back in mah car. . . ." It is a line of unbearable frenzy, zeroing in on our bones. Wright does not "interpret" it; he dishes it up, deadpan. And goes quickly on.

On one level "Big Boy Leaves Home" is the story of a single black adolescent male, his terror and victimization by a brutal community. This is the story that is the fitting first in a series of lessons on the acquisition of revolutionary power. This is the story that all the reviewers praised for its hard-boiled straight description, sticking to the facts. But the "realism" of "Big Boy Leaves Home" goes beyond Big

Boy to the psychopathology of lynching. Lynching was often
defended by white Southerners as a dramatic way of keeping
Negroes in their place—a way of keeping them from becoming "uppity." The lynching here emerges as a dramatic ceremony in which Negroes occupy the center of the sexual life
of the white community; "Big Boy" celebrates the psychic
disorder the Negro is in the white mind. The crowd
gathered to punish is a congregation assembled to worship.
And the service is indeed a *black* mass, a fertility rite in
praise of sexual destruction. The participants come away
renewed, purged, completed.

The use of dialect is rarely easy and never folksy, as it
sometimes is in Wright; it conveys a special speech, essential to the effect of such lines as "Ahll take some of yuh
ladies back in mah car." We have to hear that speech
spilling in drawl, for this story is a ghastly extravaganza on
the Southern way of life. It accomplishes what most great
stories do: its small action involves a culture, makes some
penetration into it, and tells us who the community is and
what that community's desires mean. "Big Boy Leaves
Home" is the most perfect thing Richard Wright ever wrote,
and one of the largest. It is a savage act of the mind.

CHAPTER 3

The Party

One of the funny moments (and there are a few) in Wright's essay "I Tried to Be a Communist" occurs when he describes his first "unit" meeting. After giving his report, he waits for comment, and gets only minutes of silence.

Most of the comrades sat with bowed heads. Then I was surprised to catch a twitching smile on the lips of a Negro woman. Minutes passed. The Negro woman lifted her head and looked at the organizer. The organizer smothered a smile. Then the woman broke into unrestrained laughter, bending forward and burying her face in her hands. I stared. Had I said something funny?

He asks. General giggling. What is wrong? "I did the best I could. I realize that writing is not basic or important. But, given time . . ." Still silence. He gets mad. And then later he finds out what was wrong: "I, who had been only to grammar school, had been classified as an *intellectual*. What was an intellectual? I had never heard the word used in the sense in which it was applied to me." It is a funny situation, especially if one comes to it after *Black Boy*, where on page after page all anyone can do is slap him, chase him, beat him, humiliate him. In Chicago in the early thirties the black street sweeper must have been utterly shocked to hear that word "intellectual" applied to him. A Party member draws him aside: "Intellectuals don't fit well into the Party, Wright."

But if intellectuals did not "fit well," they could be used. And Wright was used in the usual way. Daniel Aaron summarizes in *Writers on the Left*:

> The Communist writer under party discipline was expected to take on the literary assignments that would be most immediately beneficial to the revolutionary cause. The primary needs of the party were not poems or novels or critical essays; first and foremost, the party needed journalists for its press. And so, inadvertently, it became a devourer of talent (as militant parties or churches often become), transforming would-be poets and historians and novelists into producers of journalistic ephemera.

Wright produced. He was, for some months, the chief Harlem correspondent of the *Daily Worker*, writing dozens of signed articles and probably many briefer ones. It was mostly routine stuff, yet by it he grew to know the ghetto more and know it as a man responsible for telling pieces of its story. The job provided him with the raw material for fiction, as in the Angelo Herndon material for "Fire and Cloud." In an interview with Edward Strong—"Negro Youth on March, Says Leader" (October 7, 1937)—he got his epigraph for *Uncle Tom's Children*. In an article on slumlords in Harlem—"Gouging Landlord Discrimination Against Negroes Bared at Hearing" (December 15, 1937)— he had some notes for the Dalton realty policies in *Native Son*. These reports deepened his sense of the Northern urban Negro. Two years earlier, in "Joe Louis Uncovers Dynamite" (*New Masses*, October 8, 1935), he reports that after Louis knocked out Max Baer, you could sense all over South Side Chicago a feeling "of unity, of oneness" as 25,000 blacks jammed Forty-seventh Street "clasping hands" and forming "long writhing snake-lines" everywhere in "a fluid mass of joy." Wright's conclusion: "Say, Comrade, here's the wild river that's got to be harnessed and directed."

That "Say, Comrade" voice from the dark ghetto rings in most of what Wright does at this time. And it often rang in his poetry and fiction as strongly as in his journalism. Except for his adolescent thrillers like "The Voodoo of Hell's Half-Acre," he really began not as a news reporter but as an agitprop poet. That poetry has nothing to recommend it other than revolutionary enthusiasm. A typical example is "I Have Seen Black Hands," which appeared in the *New Masses*, June 26, 1934. Apparently this is a version of his very first effort, the one he describes in "I Tried to Be a Communist," the scribbled sentiments he wrote at dawn after staying up all night with his first pile of Communist pamphlets. Playing black Walt Whitman he describes all the hands and the things they've touched ("And they've held balls and bats and gloves and marbles and jack-knives and sling-shots and spinning tops in the thrill of sport and play") and then we damn the capitalists ("they jerked up and down at the throbbing machines massing taller and taller the heaps of gold in the banks of bosses") and round it off with the revolutionary threat/promise of "some red day . . . a burst of fists on a new horizon." Here and in such poems as "Rest for the Weary," "I Am a Red Slogan,"

"Strength," "I Am a Child of the Dead and Forgotten Gods" and "A Red Love Note" everything falls in on slogans. In "Red Leaves of Red Books" the hands turn and turn and finally "are hardened to the steel of unretractable purpose!" In "Spread Your Sunrise" the Russian Revolution is advised to

> Gallop on, Big Timer, gallop on!
> If anybody ask you who your Ma and Pa were
> Show your birth certificate signed by Lenin:
> UUUU! SSSS! SSSS! RRRR!

There is nothing to indicate that Wright's later judgment of these verses as "crude" was a judgment he held at the time, nor is there indication in all his writing at this period that he was sacrificing subtlety for new mass appeal. He was not writing "down" to anyone; he was writing "up" as well as he could, with a genuine enthusiasm. In these early years with the Party he continually presents the Communist as the only champion of the Negro people (see, for example, his article in the *Daily Worker,* October 25, 1937, "New Negro Pamphlet Stresses Need for U.S. People's Front," a hymn to the Party).

In "I Tried to Be a Communist" Wright plays down his association with the Party and makes it all appear rather briefer than it was. But in *Black Power* (1954) he looked back more carefully: "From 1932 to 1944 I was a member of the Communist Party of the United States of America. . . ." Richard Wright started and for over a decade persisted with the notion that his job as writer was inextricable from his job as a spokesman for the revolutionary cause. Ellison would later proclaim that "people who want to write sociology should not write a novel." But to say that is to deny the novel's traditional role with a bland assurance that "sociology" and "the novel" have nothing to do with each other. For Wright they do, very much. And his insistence in his fiction upon social commentary is usually accompanied by moral imperatives. Daniel Aaron has said that "from its beginnings, American literature has been hortatory and didactic, a literature of 'exposure,' of the first person, and although the moral tone becomes less obvious and persistent after the mid-nineteenth century, it never disappears." Wright is centrally involved in that tradition; his was to be, indeed, "a literature of 'exposure.' "

Coming up to the North he was coming from a home, a lack of a home, where no one (except for a kindly old newspaper editor) had encouraged him to become a writer or anything else. Born in one of the worst areas in the worst state, Wright suffered not only malnutrition and incessant beatings, but a vast hostility from his various foster parents, a belief that all he could do was sit on the porch and let God settle things. If he objected he got whipped, often into unconsciousness. A central appeal of the Party was not only encouragement to be something but the ecstasy of, at long last, belonging. In the "unit" for the first time he could call someone comrade. In *Black Boy* we see not only the horrors of home life but also that, by significant omission, he seems never to have had any real friends (and in all those parts of himself he would make his heroes—Big Boy, Jake Jackson, Bigger Thomas, Cross Damon, Fishbelly—each time he gives the boy a circle, usually four, of pals). In this respect Wright's experience must have been very similar to that of Angelo Herndon, who wrote that when he entered the door on the Left

all of a sudden, I had found organizations in which Negroes and whites sat together, and knew no difference of race or color. Here were organizations that weren't scared to come out for equality for the Negro people, and for the rights of the workers. The Jim-Crow system, the wage-slave system, weren't everlasting after all! It was like all of a sudden turning a corner on a dirty old street and finding yourself facing a broad, shining highway.

When Herndon decided to go down that highway his family told him not to come back, but he only said, "What did I care? My real family was the organization." That was it for Wright; here was the family denied him in Mississippi, Tennessee, and Arkansas. He found in the Party "the first sustained relationships in my life" and he was overpowered with realizing here he "could find a home."

The NAACP and other more moderate organizations were not to the point. As Wilson Record has said in *The Negro and the Communist Party,* "For literally millions of Negroes in the United States the pressing problem was not securing the franchise, justice in the courts, or admission to the colleges on an equal basis. It was one of sheer physical survival. Man did not live by bread alone, but it was hard to survive in Harlem on a dissenting opinion of Mr. Justice Brandeis." Wright, surely as much as any man in America, felt just how serious the problem was; he had lived it at its worst for over twenty years. How could he take counsel with the moderates—what did "gradualism" have to do with the waste and deprivation out of which he was coming? And what other organization really seemed to care about what happened to the Negro? In the 1930's the Party was the single agency which seemed to him to be facing the problem with adequate passion. Wright quotes a Central Committeeman, Jack Satchel, in the *Daily Worker* (August 9, 1937): "From 1919 until 1932, only one organization spoke of the class struggle. Was it the A.F. of L.? The Socialist Party? No, it was the Communist Party. It was the Communist Party that first raised the slogan for Negro rights. . . ." And who was it, after all the talk, that actually went down there with the energy and the money to *get it done* for the Scottsboro boys?

In "The Ethics of Living Jim Crow" Wright had written of a boyhood home:

Nothing green ever grew in that yard. The only touch of green we could see was far away, beyond the tracks, over where the white folks lived. But cinders were good enough for me and I never missed the green growing things. And anyhow cinders were fine weapons.

And here in the Party he seemed to be finding some "fine weapons" that he could use in the battle for revolutionary art. The Party would be his home and arsenal.

I I

Philip Rahv says the question is not whether politics is inherently good or bad for the writer: "The real question is more specific: what is the artist actually doing in politics? What is he *doing with it* and what is it *doing to him?* How does his political faith affect him as a craftsman, what influence does it exercise on the moral qualities and on the sensibility of his work?" Wright could claim in 1937 that "through a Marxist conception of reality and society . . . the maximum degree of freedom in thought and feeling can be gained for the Negro writer." A few years later he had come to feel that because his degree of freedom was minimal he would have to get out. Enough damage had been done. Aaron says, "Those who had acquired a stock of intellectual capital before enlisting as literary shock troops survived the ordeal better than did those who entered the movement without ever having undergone the apprenticeship of study and reflection. . . ."

If, in Eliot's lovely ambiguity, Henry James had "a mind so fine that no idea could violate it," Richard Wright in his twenties had a mind not at all "fine," certainly not in Eliot's sense, and an idea did violate it. The extent to which Communism did violate it can be seen in what happened when Communism lost its hold on him, when he turned frantically to other ideas, other systems, which would give him the same authority and coherence that Communism had. Other ideas again violated his art, as he bent down, bowed down, to the half-baked existentialism of *The Outsider* and the schoolbook Freud of *Savage Holiday*. Wright was particularly susceptible to schemes and systems which threatened to swallow him up. He had such feeble capacity for irony and such a passion to make the fragments of his shattered life cohere. Somewhere there *had* to be meaning.

Alfred Kazin remarked in the symposium on "The Negro in American Culture" (*Cross-Currents,* Summer 1961) that "There is a certain law for art: not to know what everything means. It's being impressed with the fact, not with the significance of the fact." Now this is surely not the "certain law for art" that Kazin claims, but it was a law for Richard Wright's art. If he started from the symbol presented to him by a system, as in *The Outsider,* the theory drowned out his capacities for liveliness, for accuracy, for truth. Where he started with a fact, his art worked best; it was not all *voulu.* Bigger Thomas is indeed a symbol, a "beast of the skull," but that symbol is no parochial one and Wright arrived at it by a lifetime of living under its pressure. No one handed it to him from Moscow or Vienna. Native Son was native. And where Wright goes wrong with that symbol of Bigger is just at the point where he exchanges his understanding of him for an "understanding" of him, the substitution of explanatory rhetoric for creative thought. As Leslie Fiedler has objected in *Love and Death in the American Novel,* "to discuss in the light of pure reason the Negro problem in the United States is to falsify its essential mystery and unreality; it is a gothic horror of our daily lives."

Protest is at the center, legitimately and successfully, of most of Wright's best work. He thinks art is a weapon. What is so wrong with all the courtroom rhetoric in the final section of *Native Son* is not that it is a weapon—the first two sections of the book are surely a weapon—but when he wants to bring out the moral of his tale Wright picks up a fake weapon and he has forgotten his target. V. S. Pritchett has said somewhere that "propaganda does not become art until it has the grace and courage to welcome the apparent defeat of its purpose." Propaganda drives in one direction and in one direction only; too much complication, intricacy, can divert us from the message. And the message is everything. Wright was innocent; he was also far too intelligent a man not to see the dangers of pat answers. But it is not difficult to see how vulnerable he was after writing the first two sections of *Native Son*. It involved such immense contradictions—and such pain—that he felt large desperation at the end. In one sense he had been too smart, had gone into it all too far. He was blinded by the intensity of his own vision, and someone had to lead him out of the cave. When the Party sent someone, how could Wright refuse his arm? That man had got black boys out of tough spots before. And as Wright reflected, so often the Party man was the only man.

The soapbox was the wrong place to stand at the end of *Native Son*, but it was the only place in the world Richard Wright could see to take his stand in 1939. In his "Blueprint for Negro Literature" he had set the responsibility upon the black writer "to furnish moral sanctions for action, to give a meaning to blighted lives, and to supply motives for mass movements of millions of people." Yet the meaning in the blighted life falls more and more out of focus as Wright concentrates more and more on the rhetoric designed to reach mass movements. And the commitment in the courtroom of *Native Son* is not so much to the black man's dilemma as it is to the Party's formulations of the Negro problem.

When he first decided to work with the Communists

Wright thought that the greatest thing he had to give them was a sense of real people and how to reach them. When his mother saw the cartoons in the *New Masses,* she "breathed in horror" at the figure of the worker holding the red flag high. She cried out, "What's wrong with that man?" Young Richard watched as she recoiled from the wild violence of the picture. She turned to him and asked, "What do Communists think people are?" After she had gone out of the room, Wright brooded, deciding that the Communists did not "quite know how to appeal to people. . . . They had a program, an ideal, but they had not yet found a language." Wright thought he had some of that language; it would be his contribution to the cause:

Here, then, was something that I could do, reveal, say. The Communists, I felt, had oversimplified the experience of those men whom they sought to lead. In their efforts to recruit masses, they had missed the meaning of the lives of the masses, had conceived of people in too abstract a manner. I would try to put some of that meaning back.

They got to him first. The quality of his language suffers severe casualties from Communist education. In his essay "Politics and the English Language" George Orwell describes the corruptions of political writing: "Prose consists less and less of *words* chosen for the sake of their meaning, and more and more of *phrases* tacked together like the sections of a prefabricated hen-house." In his political writing Richard Wright demonstrates that fault with a vengeance. He is not using words, and we can divide up the "hen-house" into its prefabricated sections:

So, let us go forth
With the determination to
STOP THE WAR,
standing ready to improvise creatively
those implements of political activity

that will wrest control
of the destiny of mankind
from the imperialist murderers and plunderers.
("Greetings," *New Masses*,
February 18, 1941, p. 41)

Or:

proceed diligently and fearlessly
to prepare the minds of millions of people
caught in the mesh of war
to answer the call
for peace when it comes.
("Not My People's War," *New Masses*,
June 17, 1941, pp. 8–9)

It is language that can be heard only through a microphone. And it comes from the man who had decided his contribution would be to give voice to "the passions of the common people." Intending to wage war against America's big lies, Wright had decided to sharpen his tools for battle. He would excel by straight talk, the unadorned colloquial idiom shooting through the platitudes of racism. But he fell into the prose of a militant, a front-line fighter, who had no time for more difficult and subtle clarities.

The language involves a special kind of platitude, clichés of violence. Wright's prose would always be one of extraordinary "drive" (he does not so much have a sense of pace as a sense of gallop), and in his hurry he fell often into mere bluster. The violence of the Party Line intensified in him a tendency that needed exactly the opposite—some sense of restraint, care, modulation. So many floodwaters had been backing up in Wright's mind; all the Party could say was "Roll, Jordan, *Roll.*" He was a black soldier in a class *struggle;* the literature was supposed to reflect the violence of that struggle, blowing apart the enemy, steaming with confrontations between workers and the police agents of the fascist oppressors. Startle, then educate. Catch the reader by his collar, hold him up off the floor, and give him a lecture. Alfred Kazin thought *Native Son* could be read not only as a Negro statement but as a typical example of literature built from the Party blueprint. The Negro Communist could "astonish the reader by torrential scenes of cruelty, hunger, rape, murder, and flight and then enlighten him by crude Stalinist homilies."

The committed literary Left wrote a prose that spews and snarls and spits. Joseph Kalar shouts down "the literary vermin that swarm over and gnaw America's literary corpse, who play the scented whore, and for thirty pieces of silver, will do the hootchi-kootchi dance. . . ." (Some vermin!) Howard Fast, whom Daniel Aaron has called "an expert practitioner of the decay-and-disease school of Communist polemic," could write of Ezra Pound's Bollingen prize: "Like a foul fistula, overloaded with pus, this corruption exploded in the presentation of the Bollingen–Library of Congress award to the fascist poet, Ezra Pound." Aaron has pointed out that in Communist pamphlets and diatribes we find continually "retch" and "vomit" and "syphilis" and "grease" and "rot" and "cancerous" (these from Party poetry).

Wright's cultural victimization by the Party is most strongly evident in the violence of his language. On the opening pages of *Native Son,* a woman's voice "sang out impatiently" and eyes are "round with fascinated horror" and "the girl whimpered" and "the woman screamed" and Vera climbed "frantically" and Bigger looked around the room "wildly" and eyes become "glued." That is, in a scene of legitimate fear—the family cowering at the presence of a giant rat—instead of making us feel it, Wright continually is *telling* us to feel it, with a pile of unnecessary adverbs, worn-out phrases, and stock poses. Wright has confessed in "How Bigger Was Born" that after over twenty tries at the opening scene he couldn't get it; one night he went out, got a bottle, and "with the help of it" he "let the rat walk in, and he did his stuff." So often in the book Wright is speaking like a man who talks "with the help" of a bottle. Yet the intoxicant that did him the greatest long-range harm was brewed by the Party. When we are told of Bigger that "his heart raced; his lips parted; his legs trembled" we hear Wright on the barricades again, whipping us up to revolutionary heat, zooming forward with the syntax of proclamation and the usual figures of stale speech: in excitement, after all, hearts race and lips part and legs do tremble. Compulsively he alliterates—in *Native Son* we have three parts: Fear, Flight, and Fate. Later he was remembering the way to get the masses with Anxiety, Ambush, and Attack in *Savage Holiday*. And in his frontal assault on the Party he was still hearing the words in the auditorium: *The Outsider* is a real feast of oratorical device, divided up into Dread, Dream, Descent, Despair, and Decision. Formal rhetorical exercise plays a major role in Wright's work—long speeches, page after page, occur in *Native Son* and *The Outsider*. He cannot get over the impulse to harangue.

When *Black Boy* was published, Wright was out of the Party; and in that book his language had broken out of the Party's spell. In scene after scene of pain, the prose just goes quietly and accurately on, coming back for more. Wright's natural province as an artist was a landscape ripped up by a gross violence; one of the hardest lessons he had to learn was that his prose would have to clarify that violence, not imitate it. The proletarian realists were incapable of teaching him that lesson; they encouraged him not to learn it.

I I I

In his years with the Communists, Wright was much more than a journalist; he became, in fact, something of a Party notable. When he replaced Horace Gregory on the board of the *New Masses,* he was feted by three hundred guests at a reception in the International Workers' Center. Then at the Third Congress of the League of American Writers he was elected to serve on the board. When the American Peace Mobilization was created in Chicago, Wright was elected a vice-president along with Theodore Dreiser, Paul Robeson, and others.

Yet, years later, he could speak of the Party synonymously with the racist system which he had once thought only the Party could destroy. Going into *Pagan Spain* he would say, "Totalitarian governments and ways of life were no mysteries to me. I had been born under an absolutistic racist regime in Mississippi; I had lived and worked for twelve years under the political dictatorship of the Communist party of the United States. . . ." In return, the Party was rough on him. As he closed the door to his "unit" he could hear voices calling him a "bastard intellectual," an "incipient Trotskyite" manifesting the "seraphim tendencies" of an "unstable personality." He was "a traitor." When he tried to march with his former comrades in a May Day Parade they lifted him and threw him "headlong through the air." "I saved myself from landing on my head by clutching a curbstone with my hands." That press which had once been lavish in his praise, that paper for which he had worked hard, now went out after him. On August 15, 1944, the *Daily Worker* ran an article by Robert Minor—"To Tell the Truth: Mr. Wright Didn't Discover It." And, most cruel, James Ford had an article on September 5 of that year—"The Case of Richard Wright: A Disservice to the Negro People."

Why did Wright decide to leave? In *Black Power* he writes that "When historic events disclosed that international Communism was mainly an instrument of Russian foreign policy, I publicly and responsibly dropped its instrumentality and dissociated myself from it." Many Negro intellectuals suspected that Communists were using them, not helping them, and one of the clearest indications was the strange snake-dance the Party performed around the American black man, going one way, another, then another. At first the Party was not opposed to Garveyism; then, by 1928, they were saying that the idea of a Negro state "must be strongly resisted." Then, by 1931, back again. The Party could not seem to decide if it really believed in its long advocacy of separate Negro nationhood (which persisted as official Party policy, in one form or another, well into the 1950's). Now calling for self-determination, then at other times calling for a complete fusion of poor blacks and poor whites, the Party was leaping back and forth across the fence. Wright would find himself asked to spur his people into the war against the Nazis, the master racists, then, after the Stalin-Hitler pact, to spur them away from it with the cry "Not My People's War." And although "Not My People's War" was prepared for the National Peace Week set to begin on June 21, 1941, it did not reach print until June 25. On June 22 Hitler's army launched a massive attack against Russia. So once again Wright had to turn about—it had become his people's war again; when *Coronet* ran a condensation of *12 Million Black Voices* he wrote a brief preface in which he supported the war. For the stage version of *Native Son* he added new lines and revised Boris Max's speech to say that Negroes wanted to play a part in any war effort that would come. But some shiftings and compromises were intolerable. When America entered the war, the Party seemed to lose sight of the black man. The Communists launched an attack on A. Philip Randolph's proposed March on Washington to demonstrate for Negro employment in defense industries. The Party said the march would be embarrassing to the President, who was concentrating on fighting fascism. The pleas of the black man would divide the country and the President's attention. And the Party announced it was not going to carry through support for Negroes who were protesting the racism of the Selective Service laws. The Party urged black people to contribute their blood to the Jim Crow blood banks.

The meaning in it all was inescapably clear. All these about-faces, pullbacks, and failures deeply disturbed Wright. The Party's behavior demonstrated no coherent and genuine concern for the Negro. Moscow's dictates were the important thing; and where the interests of the Negro conflicted with the interests of Moscow, the Party would abandon the black man.

But Wright's major objection, one that he voiced in his early essays at the time of the break, seems to have come finally from a battle that was fought on very personal grounds. What forced him out the door had ultimately to do with his sense of himself as a writer. Daniel Aaron quotes one Party member as saying that the trouble with their writers was that "they wanted to rewrite the petitions they were asked to sign." Discipline was necessary, but was that much discipline necessary? Wright asks what it was that made them all so subservient to the almighty Party that one week when an escapee from a lunatic asylum got in and started ordering everyone around on the authority of the Central Committee all the men obeyed him. What was wrong with them when a lunatic mounted an attack on one of their own comrades, whom they knew and trusted, and all began to doubt their old friend? Wright wondered, "Were we all so mad that we could not detect a madman when we saw one?"

When he went into his first "unit," Wright would say, casually, "I don't want to be organized." And as he saw more clearly the deep antagonism between political functionaries and creative individuals, he drew up his own program of "personalism." It was a kind of halfway covenant that championed "expressions of protest" but "in terms as individual and personal as possible." There seemed to be, however, no halfway of working things out with the Party. He looked around him. His comrade Joseph Freeman had been forced to suppress his book, *An American Testament,* even though it had received fine reviews upon publication. Earl Browder called Freeman in and told him Moscow condemned the book (for a passage about Trotsky). Browder said the book would have to be killed, all orders canceled, and Freeman's lecture tour put off. Leo Cherne's book, *The Rest of Your Life,* was similarly branded by Mike Gold, and the book was vilified by the Party. Wright saw that *Native Son* would have received similar treatment, for various Party heads held severe reservations about it, but the novel had been just too big a popular success for them to smear it out of existence.

Perhaps the clearest statement of the necessity to get out came when he received a letter from Antonio R. Frasconi, an artist living in Uruguay, asking advice. Frasconi had created an album of woodcuts on black people in America; his comrades in South America did not want him to publish his work. Again, the argument ran that the United States was waging an antifascist war and unity above all was the first consideration. The Frasconi-Wright exchange was eventually published in *Twice a Year* (1945). Wright answered that "Some of your advisers feel that your artistic representations of the Negro will create disunity; if that is so, then I would question seriously the kind of human unity that some of your advisers are striving to build." Wright's advice to Frasconi was to publish the work. "And I assure you that in answering your letter I have not looked at the clock in my room to see what hour of the day it is; I have

not consulted the calendar to determine the day of the
month; I have not examined a map to see where our armies
are standing. . . ." His point was clear: creative work con-
not be dependent on an ever-changing line which it is supposed to support. And Richard Wright could not work that
way, knowing that a chapter could be passed on Monday
morning and censured on Monday afternoon.

So finally Wright made the break. It was especially painful for him to leave the men who had given him so much
hope and such a sense of purpose. His devotion to the Party
had been deep. He looked back to 1938 when he had said,
"I owe my literary development to the Communist Party
and its influence, which has shaped my thought and creative
growth. It gave me my first full-bodied vision of Negro life
in America." But the Communists wanted too much, his
most precious possession, "the individual way in which I
acted and lived, an individuality which life had seared into
my bones." Too many men, with razors, with ideas, had been
demanding for too long that he hand it over. For the racists
he had only disgust; for the Communists, a deep sadness. "I
knew in my heart that I should never be able to write that
way again, should never be able to feel with that simple
sharpness about life, should never again express such passionate hope, should never again make so total a commitment of faith." But he had to go. When he writes in the
same phrase of Mississippi racism and the Communist Party
one can see why; he gradually came to see that as all the
energy of the former was ready to lynch him as a man, all
the energy of the latter could lynch him as a writer. Richard
Wright did not conceive of his writing as merely something he did. Writing was no vocation he could take up or
leave for something else. His writing was his manhood, his
assertion that he was whole. It was his sanity and his un-
destroyed self.

CHAPTER 4

The Bad Nigger

In *Black Boy* Wright tells of a Professor Matthews at the house in West Helena. Young Richard found the family gathered one night in the front room; his "Uncle" was in big trouble and the boy was terrified that this would mean they'd have to run away again. The "Uncle" had set a house on fire after knocking a woman unconscious inside. When Aunt Maggie objects that the woman would burn up, the "Uncle" replies, "I couldn't just leave her there and let somebody find her. They'd know somebody hit her. But if she burns, nobody'll ever know." Richard never found out exactly what happened, but he carried the memory of that night with him into his manhood: it would furnish him with the central event of his first and greatest literary success. In *Native Son*, Bigger Thomas accidentally smothers Mary Dalton, and then, terrified that the white folks will find the body, he decides to burn it so "nobody'll ever know."

When *Native Son* was published, as a Book-of-the-Month Club selection, it had an immediate popularity that must have astonished Wright. This was no small but satisfying work of a Negro author; *Native Son* was a national literary event. In its first month it sold a quarter of a million copies. Cass Canfield at Harper & Row said that it had started faster than any Harper novel in the previous two decades. Maybe Wright could not get banned in Boston but he was quickly banned in Birmingham (by the public library), for the implications of the story were extremely dangerous and difficult.

Wright asserted that in the act of killing, his black boy had begun to *be*. Throughout the narrative the author insisted,

It was a kind of eagerness he felt, a confidence, a fullness, a freedom; his whole life was caught up in a supreme and meaningful act.

He had murdered and created a new life for himself.

His crime was an anchor weighing him safely in time; it added to him a certain confidence. . . .

And Bigger Thomas was no Raskolnikov, no Dostoevskyan hero who at least had some massive (albeit depraved) intellectual force behind his act of killing. Bigger had no *Ubermensch* leading him on; no Idea had twisted his humanity. He killed because everything in his life had wrung humanity out of him and he only wanted to become a one-man lynch mob. He was playing Massa. Running and helpless and trapped, he suddenly crowned himself the Destroyer King. In the beginning he said on the slum streets that he would like to fly; murder presented itself as his airplane. The reviewers paid tribute to the enormous power of the narrative, but several of them questioned Wright's intellectual and moral apprehension of what that power meant. In the *Saturday Review of Literature* (March 2, 1940), Jonathan Daniels said that here was a good hard-boiled story of a rat, but it was only "the very ancient story of all criminals," not an indictment of America, for "every order creates its rats and rebels." Another critic, Charles Glicksberg, said that it was "sheer nonsense to insist that the act of killing made Bigger free, made him feel that his actions were important." Besides, Glicksberg went on, "Wright is holding a loaded pistol at the head of the white world while he mutters between clenched teeth: 'Either you grant us equal rights as human beings or else this is what will happen.' " And that is a "dangerous doctrine to pour into the susceptible minds of frustrated young Negro readers, who are resentful enough as it is." And David L. Cohn in the *Atlantic* said that Wright was exaggerating—look at how many Negroes have made a success in the United States— and Wright had succumbed to "blinding" hate worthy of the Ku Klux Klan. Ben Burns would later speak in the *Reporter* of Wright's "Hate School of Literature." Zora Hurston had complained of "Long Black Song" in *Uncle Tom's Children* that it held "lavish killing here, perhaps enough to satisfy all male black readers" and now this new novel seemed to hold enough for even the whites. Everywhere critics were objecting to the message, and everywhere people were buying the book.

In "How Bigger Was Born" Wright tries to solve some of the mysteries as to where his great "bad nigger" came from. He lists various black boys in the South whom he had known as a child, calling them Biggers 1, 2, 3, 4, and 5. Three of them were both crude and cruel, helplessly lost in

compulsive violence; two were proud, giving the whites a
dose of their own medicine. Over the years these various
boys came together, Wright said, and lay as one form, "an
undeveloped negative" that he carried with him up North,
"a negative that lay in the back of my mind." Wright seems
to say, in his essay, that it is impossible to separate legitimate
rebellion from sadism because dignity was obtainable for
his black boys only by acts of prideful destruction. His Bigger 5 pulled a knife on the conductor in a Jim Crow streetcar.
When the conductor backed down, the other Negroes in the
car "experienced an intense flash of pride." He goes farther
than that, saying that the "good niggers," the black people
in the South who had education and money—and therefore,
perhaps, a piece of the white monopoly on humanity—were
only what their names implied, "good niggers," passively
ignoring the plight of their black brothers. Wright says,
"The Bigger Thomases were the *only* Negroes I know of
who consistently violated the Jim Crow laws of the South.
. . ." (My emphasis.)

Now it is surely true that, as E. R. Embree has said,
"Richard Wright wanted to write not a book but a bomb."
And it is also true that Wright, like his fictional creation,
had an obsession with violence. Toward the end of *Black
Boy* Wright says that "it was perhaps an accident that I had
never killed." And in "How Bigger Was Born" he confesses of the Bigger 1, "Maybe I longed secretly to be like
him." Nelson Algren said in his review that "Thomas forced
recognition by an act of murder, Wright by an act of art,"
the implication being that it was very lucky Wright was able
to educate himself, to have a "socially approved" outlet for
his violence so that he could murder on paper instead of in
the flesh. And when Samuel Sillen ran a series on " 'Native
Son': Pros and Cons" in the *New Masses,* other black men
of letters came to the defense of Wright's portrait of racial

hate; Chester Himes said that Bigger "had to hate them to keep himself a human being, knowing that when he gave in to being afraid of them without hating them he would lose everything which impelled his desire to fly a plane or build a bridge." Yet Wright himself was disturbed that in the controversy too many readers and critics had been extremely careless in their understanding of what Bigger's hate meant and how he, the author, had portrayed it. Wright was moved to passionate italics in the *Atlantic* (June 1940): "No *advocacy* of hate is in that book. *None!*"

Bigger is "the beast in the skull." The difficulty in thinking clearly and talking clearly about "the beast in the skull" is that one can become so intensely, obsessively conscious of it that one lets it out, lets it out not to expose it but to let it do its damage. If one lives too long and too carelessly with the beast, one can love it. After fighting it for so long, after hating it so deeply, one feels something break inside; the hate turns to love, the fierce denial turns to passionate embrace. It is an enormously complicated problem for the black writer, trying to make sense of himself and his world. Wrestling in such agony with the beast he may begin to pump it. Becoming an intellectual Bigger Thomas, he deals in fantasies without ever seeing them for what they are. How Wright faced the problem in *Native Son* involves the question of what kind of book it is, and when one looks carefully at it one can see several indications that Wright is trying to understand the fantasy for what it is and provide some imaginative controls to direct its power.

From the very first, *Native Son* has been discussed as a specimen of naturalism. Dreiser was the name that presented itself for comparison with Wright both to Charles Poore in his review of the book for the New York *Times* and to Clifton Fadiman in the *New Yorker*. Bigger Thomas seemed something like Clyde Griffiths—both are rather unexceptional youths, forced to murders that are at least half-accidents. And in calling their books an "American" tragedy and the story of a "Native" son both Dreiser and Wright were exposing the guilt of a nation. A few years later in *Black Boy* Wright would speak of how Dreiser was one of his first, favorite authors, and also claim that "all my life had shaped me for the realism, the naturalism of the modern novel. . . ." In Dreiser as in Wright we see naturalism in its traditional form. The prose of both writers was often sloppy, hasty; their effort was not to fashion any delicate local effects but to build, to pile it on, to reach some kind of crashing force which would show us the sickness of our society.

These works followed man as if he were an animal in a laboratory, a clinical case. Dorothy Canfield Fisher called *Native Son* "The first report in fiction we have had from those who succumb to these distracting cross-currents of contradictory nerve-impulses, from those whose behavior-patterns give evidence of the same bewildered, senseless tangle of abnormal nerve-reactions studied in animals by psychologists in laboratory experiments." Wright himself would continue the metaphor in "How Bigger Was Born" by saying that he had asked himself, "Why should I not, like a scientist in a laboratory, use my imagination and invent test-tube situations, place Bigger in them. . . ."

Yet in several ways Wright's book is not like Dreiser's and it is not the "naturalism" which Dreiser wrought. As Miss Fisher said, growing restless in her "laboratory," "the novel plumbs blacker [*sic*] depths of human experience" to show "a human soul in hell because it is sick with a deadly spiritual sickness." Wright uncovers a world of grotesque symbols. He enters into that world with a furious pace and singleness that separates him from Dreiser and his scientific detachment. Bigger is not really the case for the behaviorist;

we know next to nothing about his childhood and early adolescence. Wright does not provide his "case history" in the usual naturalistic way. Irving Howe has written that in the usual naturalistic novel "the writer withdraws from a detested world and coldly piles up the evidence for detesting it." Yet *Native Son* "is a work of assault rather than withdrawal; the author yields himself in part to a vision of nightmare." Wright abandons the attempt to fashion a model of any recognizable social world.

The argument, so far, might prove no more than that naturalism is what you make it, and Wright belongs or does not belong depending on what we emphasize. If in certain respects he is unlike Dreiser, he could just as well be joined to another naturalist, Frank Norris; *McTeague* contains, like *Native Son*, a vision of nightmare full of violent murders in a surrealistic wasteland inhabited by melodramatic grotesques. And in a great many naturalist works (one thinks of Zola), the cold pile of evidence accumulates so high and with such power that "a vision of nightmare" is not an indication that the work is not naturalistic, but a logical consequence of naturalism itself.

It is not important to label the book but to understand it. While Wright drew from the naturalistic tradition, he also received another tradition, one that critics have ignored and one that may tell us a good deal about the moral and artistic economy of *Native Son*. That tradition is one of nineteenth-century American literature. Its novel has been called "Gothic" or, as Hawthorne always used it, the "Romance." To say that *Native Son* is a "Gothic Romance" is on the surface a bit tortuous—the Romance of South Side Chicago does not seem to have that much to do with "The Romance of Monte Beni"—but Wright is in league with Hawthorne and Poe in his choice of materials and in his ways of using them.

In "How Bigger Was Born" Wright comments on the scene in *Native Son* where Bigger's cell is inhabited by no less than fourteen people.

While writing that scene, I knew that it was unlikely that so many people would ever be allowed to come into a murderer's cell. But I wanted those people in that cell to elicit a certain important emotional response from Bigger. And so the scene stood. I felt that what I wanted that scene to say to the reader was *more important than its surface reality or plausibility.*

"How Bigger Was Born" was included as a preface to subsequent editions of *Native Son,* and in this regard it reminds one of Hawthorne's prefaces where he, too, comments on the improbability of some of his scenes, but hopes that the reader will let them by for "the deeper import they provide." Both authors are telling us that we must not expect the book to make sense entirely on its literal level and that we must be alert to a symbolic meaning beneath.

Wright mentions in his preface that America had "a shadow athwart our national life dense and heavy enough to satisfy even the gloomy broodings of a Hawthorne." And *Native Son* is set with familiar Hawthorne furniture: the blood, the dark basements, the guilt attendant on primitive horrors and murders. In its use of sharp, brilliant colors, blatant reds and musty blacks, Wright follows the Hawthorne pattern.

Wright was always attracted to Poe (even before the Chicago *Tribune* referred to Nixon's murder by using the phrase "the work of a giant ape" and reminding its faithful readers of "Murders in the Rue Morgue"). *Abbot's Monthly Magazine* in April of 1931 published one of Wright's very earliest works, a short story called "Superstition." It reads very much like Poe, with its ghost of beautiful Lillian and spooky echoes and general atmosphere of legendary mystery. Wright's prose echoes Poe's: "A silence fraught with the meaning of something dreadful seemed to freeze the entire room. I shall never, as long as I breathe, forget that silence." And when the silence is broken, the words could be spoken by the typical Poe figure, as Wright's character cries out "a negation of life . . . a triumph of death!" The echoes continue in *Native Son*. Wright's white cat always stalking in and circling toward Bigger is descended in all but its color (and even, in a way, in that) from Poe's black cat. The Dalton cat functions as does "The Black Cat," the furry little creature of guilt, or what the central character takes as the sign of that guilt, the cat he should have to kill or wall up before it gives him away:

The big white cat bounded down the steps and leaped with one movement upon Bigger's shoulder and sat perched there. Bigger was still, feeling that the cat had given him away, had pointed him out as the murderer of Mary.

Throughout the book there are devices and scenes which go back to the Gothic romance as it was practiced by Poe and refined by Hawthorne. There is the ghostly premonition, the sense of a curse that cannot be broken and will consume the hero (very early in the story Bigger shudders and says, "Sometimes I feel like something awful is going to happen to me"). The central symbol in the book appears early as a psychic dimension of the characters (in *Native Son* Gus and Bigger on the street corner identify "the white folks" as a feeling in the chest and throat—"It's like fire" and "sometimes you can't hardly breathe"; Bigger kills Mary by making her unable to breathe and then disposes of her in the fire). Early on, while he's watching the movie of *The Gay Woman*, Bigger thinks that maybe Mr. Dalton "had a daughter who was a hot kind of girl." Circumstantial details are all responsive to the terms of the nightmare; when Bigger walks into his predecessor's room at the Daltons', the walls are covered with pictures of "Jack Johnson, Joe Louis, Jack Dempsey, and Henry Armstrong" and also pictures of "Ginger Rogers, Jean Harlow, and Janet Gaynor"—all the men, that is, of destructive power and all but one black, all the women beautiful and white.

Native Son is a psychodrama. Hawthorne compulsively felt that he had to tell his readers to avoid quibbling about surface probabilities because he was playing a different game, trying through his symbols to embody and illuminate the terrors of history. The romance is a literary way of exploring a mysterious place, the core, the sexual center of all the cultural data that "the novel"—as opposed to "the romance"—works with in terms of everyday probability. In the Gothic romance the external details function as representations of psychic states. *The Scarlet Letter* presents a symbol of that passionate scarlet woman, that devilish woman loose in our communities, that Anne Hutchinson of our puritanical flesh and mind. Hawthorne feels a tremendous attraction to her, recovering her from the recesses of time, and he also feels a tremendous need to punish her, to pronounce a moral censure on her delinquency. *Native Son* presents the black Negro in the skull, that devilish bad nigger, toward whom Wright feels such ambivalence and whom he must project on the national scene. The romance typically works on this shifting tension between attraction and repulsion and—in Hawthorne's hands and in Wright's—ends in a fury of moralizing which points away from the true moral of the tale. D. H. Lawrence would say famously of our intensely moralistic literature, "Trust the tale, not the teller." Wright works so intently with what so drastically divides him that at the end he must deny his tale.

It may be clearer, then, why Bigger does not just kill the girl but must kill her in a special way. Don Stanford objected in the *Southern Review* (Winter 1940) that while

Native Son was "a fine psychological study of race hatred" it was "marred by two unnecessarily brutal murders." And David Daiches in *Partisan Review* (Spring 1940) said the same: *Native Son* was a good book, a very good book, but the violence was "fortuitous," too "melodramatic," and interfered with the "illustrative fable" because it is "not the kind of action" such men are "likely" to be driven to. But surely these objections miss Wright's central point and the function of his central methods. Wright goes to the center of the racial nightmare and attempts to understand it in terms of thwarted sexuality. When Bigger beheads Mary, "the gleaming metal reflected the tremulous fury of the coals. Yes; he *had* to. Gently, he sawed the blade into the flesh and struck a bone. He gritted his teeth and cut harder. As yet there was no blood anywhere but on the knife." It is a scene of sexual violation, a man breaking into a woman, and Bigger at first acts—that incredible adverb—"gently." When the maiden's head goes off, we see "the curly black hair . . . in blood." As Bigger leaves, the image floats up in his head of Jan and Mary lying in the back seat. At home, satisfied, released, he falls immediately asleep. He has had her. And no one else will, ever again.

To present such a scene is, of course, extraordinarily dangerous, and Wright thought about it with extreme hesitation. He had complained in 1937 that too many Negro works were "prim and decorous Ambassadors who went a-begging to white America" all dressed up "in the knee-pants of servility, curtseying to show that the Negro was not inferior. . . ." Here he had not made that mistake. But he might have made another. Baldwin was later to complain in "Many Thousands Gone" that to write such a scene as the beheading of Mary Dalton was only "to whet the notorious national appetite for the sensational" and such violence was "gratuitous and compulsive." While Wright "recorded, as no Negro before him had ever done, that fantasy Americans hold in their minds when they speak of the Negro," nevertheless, "to present Bigger as a warning is simply to reinforce the American guilt and fear concerning him." In *Native Son* "we find here merely, repeated in anger, the story which we have told in pride." The same objection was voiced by Theodore Solotaroff in his "Afterword" to the Signet paperback reprint of *Native Son* in 1964, when he said that "the immediate effect of Wright's melodrama is to revitalize prejudices and projections on both sides and to contribute to the apocalyptic aura that inflames the imagination of our crisis but distracts from and weakens an understanding of it."

Yet Wright himself was well aware of the danger he was running. In "How Bigger Was Born" he shows how deeply he knew that such a book could "revitalize prejudices and projections on both sides" (Solotaroff) and "reinforce the American guilt and fear" (Baldwin). Wright asked himself: "What will white people think if I draw the picture of such a Negro boy? Will they not at once say: 'See, didn't we tell you all along that niggers are like that? Now, look, one of their own kind has come along and drawn the picture for us!'" Wright presents the various objections from all sides, then finally turns them down. Or, rather, Bigger himself turns them down: "Bigger won over all these claims; he won because I felt that I was hunting on the trail of more exciting and thrilling game." *Native Son*, then, would be a big-game hunt, Wright would go out on imaginative safari for the man-eater, the "beast in the skull," try to find him and kill him first.

Wright provides us with artistic and moral equipment to understand that hunt as more than an outraged repetition of a stereotype. Of key importance is that sense of psychodrama, that the surface reality is a way of getting to a psychic reality. These things are true *in the head,* in the mind of history. Each of the three times Bigger kills he goes for the head. In the first scene, when he throws the skittle at the rat, he is "cursing hysterically" while he crushes its skull. Mary he smothers, a pillow over her head, and then in the basement he beheads her. And when he kills Bessie in the abandoned apartment building he pounds time after time at her head with the brick. His terror and hate of the head comes home to him in one of his nightmares:

He had a big package in his arms so wet and slippery and heavy that he could scarcely hold onto it and he wanted to know what was in the package and he stopped near an alley corner and unwrapped it and the paper fell away and he saw—it was his *own* head—his own head lying with black face and half-closed eyes. . . .

Throughout, the physical description that Wright rushes by us makes us feel the emotional force of the objects but not see them with any real accuracy: we are aware of the furnace and storm as poles of the imagination—fire and ice—in a world of symbolic presences. Continually the world is transformed into a kind of massive skull, and the people are figments of that skull's imagination. Hawthorne's Pyncheon house was an asymmetrical, grotesque image of the Pyncheon sensibility; just as Poe's house of Usher had its great central crack that would make it "Fall," the schizophrenia that finally splits and kills Roderick Usher. In *Native Son* Bigger sees the houses of the black ghetto as great heads. With Bessie he sees a "snow-covered building whose many windows gaped blackly, like the eye-sockets of empty skulls." And when Bigger lives alone and terrified in the skull of one of those buildings he is playing out his role, consistently symbolized throughout the book, as an occupant of our imagination, a man imprisoned in our minds. Wherever he turns, trying to break open heads, he wants to get out of the mental cage. Wright's insistence on the image presents the violence as an act of the imagination, turning to the terms of its imprisonment, and insistently reminding us, through those key terms, that what is going on here is a psychic struggle, an act of imaginative liberation.

All of which says, finally, that *Native Son* is no more a Gothic romance than it is a naturalistic novel. The Gothic romance involves a complicated relationship between the creative imagination and the external world and establishes a distance between them which *Native Son* simply does not, in any formal way, observe. Hawthorne goes back, in his greatest success, two hundred years; we participate in his imaginative recapturing of the past. There is a certain stability in Hawthorne's sense of that past and a certain assurance in his setting up of the key signs and interpreting them. Poe creates extremities of consciousness, aberrations, but only while showing us that that is what they are. He makes his extremes on his own terms. In both Hawthorne and Poe we have the sense of a conscious manipulation of the materials, a willful departure from actuality and a distortion of it to get back to the truth that actuality had hidden from us.

Wright had no possibility of any settled distance; the willful distortions of Hawthorne and Poe were forced upon Wright by the dominant culture. One of the reasons Wright could not fashion a Gothic romance was most clearly stated by Wright himself in the last sentence of his essay "How Bigger Was Born." All through that final paragraph Wright talks of James and Hawthorne and Poe, their relationship to the American scene, and then concludes that paragraph and his essay with a perception that shows us more clearly than anything else how his problem was different from theirs: "And if Poe were alive, he would not have to invent horror; horror would invent him." The nineteenth-century writers could erect fantasies in the head; Wright was trying to rid himself of the fantasy in his.

In "Bright and Morning Star" the final scene is one of unbearable horror; the old Negro mother keeps begging the white men to shoot her son so he won't suffer, but they only break his legs over a log, crunching the kneecaps with a crowbar, and then split his eardrums, "his eyes showing white amazement in a world without sound." That last phrase recurs in *Native Son* not in a scene of a black man being mutilated but in a scene where a black man remembers how he mutilated a white woman: suddenly the winter fields around Bigger burst into "a world of magic whiteness without sound." The change is from the black man being killed to the black man killing. Similarly, after the imagined sexual transgression, the whites of "Big Boy Leaves Home" mutilate and burn the Negro boy; in *Native Son,* after the fear that he will be accused of sexual transgression, the black boy mutilates and burns the white body. In this way the sales figures of *Native Son* are not so surprising; it is a book that the whites already know about, the story of their guilt, but it is a shocking new report from the other side of their own wall.

A stereotype is not an archetype. *Native Son* leads us into myth, taking a common assumption of the culture and elaborating it in so accurate and energetic a way that the culture finds in it the expression of one of its deepest drives. Bigger Thomas is a legendary figure of the Western mind, belonging with figures like Robinson Crusoe, Bigger embodying as successfully the Myth of Race as Crusoe embodies the Myth of Individual Enterprise. James Baldwin's struggle with Bigger is an intensely moving one to watch; while Baldwin cannot relax his rage, he is far too intelligent to let anyone bully him into false terms. Yet I think the answer to his repeated objection (that Wright only reinforces stereotypes and repeats them in fury) will have to come from the fact, simply, that no white man could have written *Native Son*. The extraordinary quality of the book is its "niggerness." Here the black man is struggling to release himself by beating the white man at his own game. Wright may not be able to write the romance, but in many ways he is like Hester Prynne in Hawthorne's most famous one: cast out of the community, branded with a terrible letter (skin) of shame, he wears it proudly. Hester's embroidery of her symbol and Wright's assertion of his Biggerness is a way of wearing proudly the shame the culture lays down; it is a way of taking the terms and fighting back. Wright could not assert *Négritude,* for it was not historically available; he could assert his niggerhood, and he could do it in such a way that the stereotype would be lifted into myth.

Wright said that finally his choice to write the book came when he decided, "I must write this novel, not only for others to read, but to free *myself* of this sense of shame and fear. In fact, the novel, as time passed, grew upon me to the extent that it became a necessity to write it; the writing of it turned into a way of living for me." Wright was creating and living every day with his beast in the skull, Bigger, the psychopath. Norman Mailer has written in "The White Negro" that:

Many people with a psychoanalytical orientation often confuse the psychopath with the psychotic. Yet the terms are polar. The psychotic is legally insane, the psychopath is not; the psychotic is almost always incapable of discharging in physical acts the rage of his frustration, while the psychopath at his extreme is virtually as incapable of restraining his violence.

And the creation of Bigger Thomas, for Richard Wright, was to get at the psychopath in himself, his twisted roots and frantic edges. Mailer goes on in his famous essay to suggest that such an artist must go "exploring backward along the road" of all the rape and robbery and murder, all the real or potential crimes, in order "to find those violent parallels to the violent and often hopeless contradictions he knew as an infant and as a child . . . and so free himself to remake a bit of his nervous system." Wright was, as his anguished statements in "How Bigger Was Born" make clear, engaged in just this task. Exorcism. Which is not at all merely to repeat a stereotype but a way of exploring the empirical truths of the passions that sustain the stereotype. A stereotype could not exist if it did not have something to do with the truth; if the stereotype does not offer some accuracy about a people or the way we feel about a people, it would cease to have imaginative currency. Further, the stereotype separates a man from himself. A man cannot find himself because the stereotype interferes by insisting that his category is more than his individuality. In *Native Son* Wright attempts to destroy the cliché by giving it its full imaginative due.

He would say in "I Bite the Hand That Feeds Me" (*Atlantic,* June 1940), "I wrote *Native Son* to show what manner of men and women our 'society of the majority' breeds, and my aim was to depict a character in terms of the living tissue and texture of daily consciousness." In that way, because he was able to do that, he was able to give white Americans the bad nigger—whom they knew—but he was also able to give those readers Bigger Thomas—whom they did not know. However desperate, it is an act of creation. In *The Wretched of the Earth* Fanon advised the militant black intellectual that sometimes he would have to "will to be a nigger, not just a nigger like all other niggers but a real nigger, a Negro cur, just the sort of nigger the white man wants. . . ." Someone, say, like Bigger Thomas. Richard Wright, so contemptuous of those "prim and decorous Ambassadors" in assimilationist Negro literature, was pulling out of himself and pushing onto the page "just the sort of nigger the white man wants." For centuries the white community had been standing on top of the world shouting down into the cave, "We know you're down there, we know you're down there." Small wonder the white world shrank back when the growl came up:

"Ah, but I am."

II

In his essay on Bigger's birth, Wright said that "life had made the plot over and over again, to the extent that I knew it by heart." Repeatedly he had seen black boys picked off the streets to be charged with an unsolved case of "rape." "This thing happens so often that to my mind it had become a representative symbol of the Negro's uncertain position in America." Robert Nixon was apprehended and sent sprawling across the front page of the *Tribune* while Wright was in mid-passage with Bigger Thomas. The actual case is a part of history—as the novel is part of the literary history—of the thing itself. In Chicago in 1938 two black men were testifying to the myth, one with a brick and the other with a book.

Richard, like Bigger, lived in a Chicago slum with his mother. As an insurance agent Wright had visited various black kitchenettes like the one with which his book would begin. In the opening scene the people driven so closely together are driven violently apart. Wright would say the following year, in *12 Million Black Voices*, "The kitchenette throws desperate and unhappy people into an unbearable closeness of association, thereby increasing latent friction, giving birth to never-ending quarrels of recrimination, accusation, and vindictiveness, producing warped personalities." The full recognition of how the "kitchenette" (which

refers to the cramped apartment itself, not just the cook-
ing area) forms Bigger's sensibility—or how it deprived him
of what we could call a "sensibility"—was one of Wright's
most daring and significant choices.

In "Many Thousands Gone," Baldwin saw that "Bigger
has no discernible relationship to himself, to his own life,
to his own people, nor to any other people" and because
of that "a necessary dimension has been cut away." But that
was surely Wright's point; he knew that he was cutting
away a dimension. He said in "How Bigger Was Born" that
he planned for his black boy to be "estranged from the
religion and the folk culture of his race"—a statement that
shows that Wright was consciously pulling things away and
not, as the criticism against Wright might lead one to believe, that Wright just didn't know how to show them. In
12 Million Black Voices he summarized:

Perhaps never in history has a more utterly unprepared folk
wanted to go to the city; we were barely born as a folk when we
headed for the tall and sprawling centers of steel and stone.
We, who were landless on the land; we, who had barely managed to live in family groups; we, who needed the ritual and
guidance of institutions to hold our atomized lives together in
lines of purpose; we, who had known only relationships to
people and not relationships to things; we, who had never
belonged to any organizations except the church and burial
societies; we, who had had our personalities blasted with two
hundred years of slavery and had been turned loose to shift
for ourselves. . . .

In the figure of Bigger Thomas, Wright was trying to show
the ultimate sense of horror: unpreparedness set loose in a
metropolis. Bigger has nothing to hold him back and
nothing to define his responses other than the blackness of
his skin. He is, as his mother wails, "black crazy"; his mind
is crazed by his color. He is incapable of a nonracial thought.
His obsession produces what Wright would later call, "The

State of Exaggeration." In *White Man, Listen!,* Wright says that "one of the aspects of life of the American Negro that has amazed observers is the emotional intensity with which he attacks ordinary, daily problems." How can the mind ever relax or grow when its defining problem is always and unbearably one thing? Wright offers as an example the problem a Negro has in renting a place to live; the over-riding question, the one that gathers all the usual questions of whether the place is clean, whether it is well-made, whether it's near a school, whether it's near stores, is only one question: can a black person live there? And as the great migration moved northward in the twenties and thirties the black folk found their answer. They would live in the kitchenette.

This "state of exaggeration" that Wright speaks of is most clearly seen in the kitchenette by an overwhelming fear of being looked at. The kitchenette means lack of privacy. On the first page of *Native Son,* when people get out of bed, the first words are "Turn your heads so I can dress." Day after day in the ghetto that is the call to society; and on the second day of Wright's story, in the center sec-tion of his book, Vera repeats the line "Turn your head so I can dress." Even when one is dressed, the fear continues at the breakfast table, this horror of being seen.

> "Stop looking at me, Bigger!"
> "Aw, shut up and eat your breakfast!"
> "Ma, make 'im stop looking at me!"
> "I ain't looking at her, Ma!"
> "You *is!*" Vera said.

And so it goes, on into the night where children are given their sexual education because the mother and father cannot not give it to them. After his murders Bigger roams the ghetto apartment houses, climbing them and peering into windows where he sees through a window without shades . . . a room in which were two small iron beds with sheets dirty and crumpled. In one bed sat three naked black children looking across the room to the other bed on which lay a man and woman, both naked and black. . . . There were quick, jerky movements on the bed where the man and woman lay, and the three children were watching.

Bigger sees it as a memory, for he, too, had often "awakened and watched his father and mother." He climbs on up with one last look in at "the man and woman moving jerkily in tight embrace, and the three children watching."

Wright's point is not to deny the Negro's "folk culture." He was trying to show that for these urban slum dwellers the folk culture was swallowed in unbearable closeness. This emptiness and fear of being looked at Bigger carries with him all the day long. The scene which begins the book is present at the very center of the crime where Bigger is hysterical at not being able to get the full human form into a tight place. He has to cut off the head. Bigger's head, his sensibility, was cut off in the kitchenette. (And the severed head appears in his dream as his own.) At the end of the book Max keeps asking Bigger what Mary Dalton had done to him that made Bigger say, "I ain't sorry she's dead." Bigger struggles for the answer; all he knows is that he hated her. He stammers and tries to find it and then vaguely he gets an image of his sister

Vera, sitting on the edge of a chair crying because he had shamed her by "looking" at her; he saw her rise and fling her shoe at him. He shook his head confused.

That is it: racial misery is indecent exposure.

And so Wright would tell us at the beginning of his story that Bigger's relationship to his family was that "he lived with them, but behind a wall, a curtain." When he relates to black people he takes his violence out on them. His hate

bottles up and has to get out; since it cannot reach its stim-
ulus, the white man, it is expelled on blacks. He corners
his pal, Gus, and holds a knife blade at his mouth, saying,
"Lick it." What he wants to do, of course, is hold it at the
white man's lips, draw blood from the white man's tongue.
But he can't get at him. Bigger "had heard it said that white
people felt it was good when one Negro killed another; it
meant that they had one Negro less to contend with." When
a Negro says he is afraid to go to Mississippi because "down
there they'd as soon kill you as look at you" he does not refer
merely to the white race. Bigger cannot feel "guilt" about
his murders. His is a mind in which "guilt" plays as neg-
ligible a part as it did in the whites who set fire to Bobo.
Bigger cannot say, "I have killed a *human being*," for there
are no human beings on his planet. Bessie was not at all
his "sweetheart," only the "girl" he had because other boys
had them. His relationship to her is his relationship to
the black community; he will use and enjoy her when he
can and strike out when she gets in his way. "The black
girl was merely 'evidence.' And under it all he knew that the
white people did not really care about Bessie's being killed."

Bigger is, then, one of the Negro's "roles" (in spite of
the continuing objection that he is not) and the white
reader can see it more clearly now as black voices from the
ghetto begin to come out with verification of how accurate
Bigger was. Anyone who has read *The Autobiography of
Malcolm X* or *Manchild in the Promised Land* or Eldridge
Cleaver's remarkable *Soul on Ice* can see Biggers in the
characters the authors draw around them and explore, with
considerable courage, in themselves. Wright does not, as
Baldwin said, "cut a necessary dimension away." Again,
white America beat him to it. Had Wright not portrayed
Bigger in this way he would have been cutting a "necessary
dimension away" not from his figure but from the im-

portance of the forces that would make him what he was. To create a "folk tradition" in the slum—that is, to create whole human beings in a brutally fragmented world—would not be to take that world seriously. It would be a gross underestimation of how massive the damage is. Wright saw that if people do not have any chance to get culture it is rather unlikely that they will have its blessings.

When Bigger goes out onto the street he sees a poster for Buckley's campaign: "IF YOU BREAK THE LAW, YOU CAN'T WIN!" And, as Bigger knows, if you don't break it, you keep losing. This is the white man's law. What Bigger has available to him is no "folk tradition" but the glittery expression of the white civilization. He goes to a movie, *The Gay Woman,* in which he gets that tradition in "scenes of cocktail drinking, dancing, golfing, swimming, and spinning roulette wheels, a rich young white woman kept clandestine appointments with her lover while her millionaire husband was busy in the offices of a vast paper mill." If Bigger went to that world of money and fancy sex, the white folks would run—thinking, as Bigger's chum says, "a gorilla broke loose from the zoo and put on a tuxedo."

When Bigger actually goes into the white mansion where "the gay woman" lives, he goes as a chauffeur. His position behind the wheel is a gross parody of his deepest wish: to be behind the stick of the airplane. Passionate to get out of his prison, to roam the skies, he is only a "driver." Bigger is constantly assuming such poses that are emblematic stances of the Negro. When he puts the white maiden in the trunk and carries her down to the furnace he is frozen for a moment as the jolly redcap at the station. The black destroyer is a porter. Climbing buildings he is the giant darky we blew up onto the screen, the "Bigger" black man; he stands roaring on the rooftops until white technology sends him plummeting to the street below. And *King Kong* ends with the assertion that "beauty killed the beast" just as *Native Son* shows how the beast—if given a chance—will kill the beauty.

The scene with Jan and Mary is one of gross comedy. In order to make Bigger feel at home Jan says first of all in the restaurant, "You like fried chicken?" (And decades later Lenny Bruce would begin his sketch, "How to Make a Negro Feel Comfortable at a Party" with the white host going over to the black guest—"Can I get you something? Piece of watermelon? Chicken leg?") Jan and Mary are locked almost as tightly in stereotypes as is Bigger. The drunker they get the more they retreat into those stereotypes, and Mary asks Bigger to sing "Swing low, sweet chariot, Coming fer to carry me home. . . ." Fer, she says. All of it is torture for Bigger, who at the beginning was so impressed with them and so upset that he couldn't stop saying "*yessuh* and *yessum* to white people in one night when he had been saying it all his life long." In the early hours he could not eat with them because under the pressure of their openness he could not chew; it seemed to him "that the very organic functions of his body had altered." As the game goes on he cannot escape the suspicion that they are playing a dreadful game with him, cheating him of the stability, the certainty, that he has learned.

When the Daltons wanted to "give the negroes a chance," they never reckoned with just how well Bigger would take it. The game that Jan and Mary play throws off his timing. He never wanted to know people like Jan ("He didn't want to meet any Communists. They didn't have any money") and now he has known for too long that whites are not people. "He was sitting between two vast white looming walls." When the walls talk, and ask him, "We seem strange to you, don't we, Bigger?" he replies, "Oh, no'm," and the female wall gets mad. Bigger keeps using the language that's supposed to work, he keeps trying not to be noticed. These whites are cheating; they made up the game and now they're not sticking to the rules. "These people made him feel things he did not want to feel." He has a right to be suspicious; when she gets enough rum, Mary begins to hold him up for amusement. Come, driver, do your tricks.

When he kills, his only way of apprehending that death is: "She was dead; she was white; she was a woman; he had killed her; he was black. . . ." It is part of the general stunting of his emotional growth. He later enjoys reports of Japan's war on China and the news that Hitler is "running the Jews to the ground" and Mussolini's troops are slaughtering Spain. There is never any "moral" question for him; aggressions and atrocities are a way of getting out of racial pain. All he wants is some day some black man "who would whip the black people into a tight band and together they would act and end fear and shame." He lives in a world where guilt can only be "a white blur" of blind Mrs. Dalton.* Guilt is no more than terror; when he sees "the awesome white blur floating toward him" he kills the whiteness.

The murder is an act of creation. It is a way of escaping all the negatives in his life: "The knowledge that he had killed a white girl they loved and regarded as their symbol of beauty made him feel the equal of them, like a man who had been somehow cheated, but had now evened the score." He has had *The Gay Woman,* the pretty white girl who gets drunk. He has taken her out of her high room,

---

* David B. Davis has suggested to me an interesting version, possibly a source, for this central dramatic scene involving Bigger, Mary, and the blind mother. In Thomas Dixon's *The Clansman,* 1905 (on which *Birth of a Nation,* the first Hollywood spectacular, was based), the insufferable blond virgin, Marion, is raped by the young black man, Gus (the name of Bigger Thomas's best buddy). The rapist's identity is later discovered by a "scientific" study of his image in the eye of the mother, who watched her daughter's violation.

brought her down to his own level. He has had her on his bed of coals. Bigger had "committed rape every time he looked into a white face" and now he has done it in a way that the white face would have to cry out in pain. He creates by making whole, by severing the perpetual discontinuity between his two worlds, his aspirations and his abilities to attain their satisfaction; "never had he felt a sense of wholeness" until he introduced Mary Dalton to the furnace.

Murder is a recapitulation of suffering. Bigger hides in empty houses the way Big Boy hid in empty kilns. Bigger wants to know "the right way" to behave when he is captured, "the right way being the way that would enable him to die without shame"—as in *Uncle Tom's Children* Brother Mann and especially Silas in "Long Black Song" and the Negro mother in "Bright and Morning Star" wanted to die. In this sense *Native Son* becomes a way of retrieving the pain of *Uncle Tom's Children,* hurtling that pain into the white community.

But Bigger's act is as futile as was any of the acts in *Uncle Tom's Children* and can bring only the same results. As soon as the newspaper can run the headlines "AUTHORITIES HINT SEX CRIME," Bigger knows it is all over. He has blown the fuse in the white mind. Immediately the police are able to gather three thousand volunteers. "The Negro rapist and murderer" the papers call him before he gets a chance. Massive reprisals come immediately and hundreds of black employees are fired from their jobs, Negro men are beaten on the streets, and all the ghetto hot spots are raided and closed down. The triumph must yet again remain in the mind.

Wright's novel begins to fall slightly out of focus as he tries to show how that triumph registers in his hero's mind.

Bigger is smart. The problem Wright did not adequately solve was the nature of Bigger's intelligence. For the most part we see it as a strategic, military mind; he feels power and knows how to use it. But he has no "ideas"—just the vast obsession. He can see the world only as "iron palms" and "fiery furnaces" and a "sea of white faces," blurs of motion and sound and racial horrors. Yet Wright begins to dress up Bigger's "act of creation" in a prose that rings false. Bigger had "accepted the moral guilt and responsibility for that murder"—but he had not; he could not think in terms of "moral guilt and responsibility," let alone "accept" them. When "a supreme act of will springing from the essence of his being" drove him into crime he "looked wistfully upon the dark face of ancient waters upon which some spirit had breathed and created him." The language is all wrong, and so is Bigger. Preparing for the forensics in the courtroom, Wright begins to lose his grasp on his great character. Able to "look wistfully upon the dark face of ancient waters" Bigger can see a gavel in the courtroom only as a "hammerlike piece of wood."

The problem had been with Wright from the beginning, and all along he had been wrestling with it. In the second section, "Even though Mr. Dalton gave millions of dollars for Negro education, he would rent houses to Negroes only in this prescribed area, the corner of the city tumbling down from rot. In a sullen way Bigger was conscious of this." Wright wants to make his point, then suddenly realizes how important it is that we see it only through Bigger's eyes, and so he leans on "a sullen way" of consciousness. As Bigger climbs in the abandoned house "he remembered that bombs had been thrown by whites into houses like these when Negroes had first moved into the South Side"—yet while Bigger might know that, he does not "remember" it as he climbs inside the old wreck.

The fuzziness in Bigger's characterization is part of a general falling off in the third part as the terms of the book begin to change. Bigger is undergoing a psychic rehabilitation, and too often we see him in his Sunday best: "He lay on the cold floor sobbing; but really he was standing up strongly with contrite heart. . . ."

Margaret Butcher has summed up the usual objection voiced against the third part of Wright's novel. "Ideological commitment cheated him of a classic." The Party had interrupted Wright's project and falsified the message of "the bad nigger." Wright himself said in "How Bigger Was Born":

Two items of my experience combined to make me aware of Bigger as a meaningful and prophetic symbol. First, being free of the daily pressure of the Dixie environment, I was able to come into possession of my own feelings. Second, my contact with the labor movement and its ideology made me see Bigger clearly and feel what he meant. I made the discovery that Bigger Thomas was not black all the time; he was white, too, and there were literally millions of him, everywhere.

Wright seems to want Bigger to stand for any colorless slum kid; his problems are the problems of any impoverished group. Yet in the last section of *Native Son* this idea is only presented briefly and parenthetically in Boris Max's speech. When it makes its second appearance, in the very last scene in the prison cell, Max draws Bigger to the little barred window, shows him the skyscrapers, and says that *that* is what killed you, Bigger, the capitalist economy; the men in those buildings "want to keep what they own, even if it makes others suffer." But Bigger rejects all that. He knows the problems of his life cannot be explained by economics or the class system. Bigger knows, however crudely, what kind of skull he is in.

For the most part, in his lengthy courtroom address, Max

takes the terms for granted and speaks solely to the problem of race. What is wrong in the courtroom is not this evasion of the problem by an assertion that "Bigger was not black all the time." Something more generally is wrong with the entire idea of a courtroom confrontation itself. The name "Bigger Thomas" carries us back to the name in that other famous novel which had achieved such immediate and large sales almost a century before. Bigger Thomas is "bigger" than Uncle Tom, but he is part of the family, a son, just as Tom was an uncle. And Wright will use some of Mrs. Stowe's imagery for the Negro in America. The black man is Christ; he is Christ in the complicated way that Buckley, State's Attorney, impulsively feels when he cries, "O suffering Christ, there are no words to tell of a deed so black and awful!" (that is, an inverted Christ). When Bigger is captured, "two men stretched his arms out, as though about to crucify him." The black Christ is nailed by white America. James Baldwin saw *Native Son* as "a continuation, a complement of that monstrous legend it was written to destroy," for in Wright's book

Bigger is Uncle Tom's descendant, flesh of his flesh, so exactly opposite a portrait that, when the books are placed together, it seems that the contemporary Negro novelist and the dead New England woman are locked together in a deadly, timeless battle; the one uttering merciless exhortations, the other shouting curses.

Mrs. Stowe often sacrificed her characters to the moral crusade; the fictional personages became mere pawns in the propagandistic enterprise. The figure of St. Clare is well drawn in the first part of the book, but he tends to disintegrate into merely a mouthpiece for high-sounding morals. That is what begins to happen in Wright's courtroom. Max's speech falls into the category. Mrs. Stowe wrote her book, she said, "to awaken sympathy for the African race as they exist among us," and what else is Boris Max trying to do? Mrs. Stowe showed it by Uncle Tom's gigantic loveliness, concluding we should not do horrid things to people like that. Max shows Bigger's enormous sickness, concluding he is sick because the society is. From exactly opposite directions the two avenues come to the same destination: the crusader tells white America to stop ruining black people.

In the first two parts of the book Wright had been doing something intensely more complicated. We were not seeing Bigger as an object; we were participating with him as a subject. No white man could have written that part of the book, no white man could have stayed so resolutely and utterly in Bigger's brain. But a white man could have written all the courtroom speeches (and it is a white man who gives them). In the last section we are no longer in Bigger's mind. He continues to be the zero he was at the beginning of that third book, a brute in a chair, only listening. Max asks, "Let me, Your Honor, explain further the meaning of Bigger Thomas' life." That is exactly the flaw. I have said the chief virtue of the novel is that it is an exorcism, a calling up of mysterious disasters; the chief error of the third part of the novel is that it is only explanation, no longer a vital artistic effort at a full understanding. What Max is saying is surely true, but it is a truth of a far less demanding kind, the lesser truth that Mrs. Stowe herself achieved.

Your Honor, consider the mere physical aspect of our civilization. How alluring, how dazzling it is! How it excites the senses! How it seems to dangle within easy reach of everyone the fulfillment of happiness! How constantly and overwhelmingly the advertisements, radios, newspapers and movies play upon us! But in thinking of them remember that to many they are tokens of mockery. These bright colors may fill our hearts with elation, but to many they are daily taunts. Imagine a man walking amid such a scene, a part of it, and yet knowing that it is *not* for him!"

All of this is certainly true, not at all an extraneous interpretation of the action. It is a perfectly accurate description
of what the action can show us. That is what is wrong. It
is an "interpretation." It is part of Wright's flaw of over-
writing, a consequence of his fear that we will not see
Bigger's meaning, and he must rush in to point it out to us.
The third section of the book, all the rhetoric in the courtroom, is the architectural equivalent of the local failures
all through the book sentence by sentence, in the unnecessary adverbs and stereotypic figures of speech.

When Bigger is attacked in court, beaten in the head, he
is going through a torture that Wright had read about in
the Robert Nixon case. On June 8, 1938, Elmer Johnson,
the husband of Florence, smashed his fists into Nixon's face
at the inquest. Later Nixon rushed Johnson on the stand
and tried to strangle him. Thus, at Nixon's trial, and at
Bigger's, the courtroom is ringed with uniformed guards to
keep the people apart. All of this Wright is able to convey
convincingly. But the performance of the lawyer is incredibly stupid—if he is supposed to be a lawyer concerned with
getting his man off, and not just a mouthpiece.

The relationship between the Thomas family and the Dalton
family was that of renter to landlord, customer–merchant, em-
ployee to employer. The Thomas family got poor and the
Dalton family got rich. And Mr. Dalton, a decent man, tried to
salve his feelings by giving money. But, my friend, gold was
not enough! Corpses cannot be bribed! Say to yourself, Mr.
Dalton, "I offered my daughter as a burnt sacrifice and it was
not enough to push back into its grave this thing that haunts
me."

How Bigger is going to be assisted by this line is utterly un-
clear. Those people in the jury box, staring at the father of
the lost child, hear her described as a burnt offering; to
see Dalton browbeaten will not impel them to leniency.
The passage also distracts us and exposes as obtrusive and

mechanical the symbols we had lived through with Bigger.
It is "poetic justice"—and no other kind—that the Thomas
house should be owned by the Daltons. All perfectly true,
of course—the philanthropist gouged the rent out of the
Negroes and paid them back with ping-pong tables—but we
could get that on the pages of the *Daily Worker* and it is an
insane tactic in a courtroom. The lawyer turns to the poor
blind mother: "And to Mrs. Dalton, I say: 'Your philan-
thropy was as tragically blind as your sightless eyes!' " Again,
the defense attorney is publicly badgering a defenseless
blind parent weeping for the lost child. The "blindness" of
Mrs. Dalton had been a great dramatic touch, for we felt
Bigger's fear of it, his sense that she was compensating for
it with some supersensory perception that saw into him
as other whites could not. Her blindness had been an important key in the plot; she had to be in the room, but
unable to see, for the accidental murder to take place. But
the critic who praises the book for its symbols ("a constant
play on blindness, focused around the figure of Mrs. Dalton
but aimed ultimately at the reader") is taking the least demanding of Wright's terms.

When we are pulled up out of the nightmare to this reflection upon it, we begin to ask all the wrong questions.
The rum bottle—how does it suddenly appear in court when
Jan had left it in the gutter and there was no reason for
anyone to start looking for it until several days and several
garbage trucks had passed? When the judge calls the lawyers
forward and they have a conference at "the railing" for
"over an hour" surely in any courtroom the conference
would be in the judge's chambers. These are silly little details, hardly worth mention, but they bother us in the third
part because we are "shedding daylight" on the problem—
we have gone out of Bigger's mind to look back on it—and
the book comes to a standstill, where we look at the land-

scape to see everything out of place. Max is not defending
Bigger; Wright is using Max to point Bigger's tragedy out.

Bigger has, as one critic has said, an "incurable neurosis."
Or, as Wright himself said, Bigger is "an obscene joke happening." In one sense the courtroom scene is in a line of
the finest detective stories and murder mysteries, Wright's
attempt to take the step that will lead to greatness. He is
trying to expose communal guilt. He is entering on a question of judgment that will judge the whole structure of his
work and the moral views we hold of it. We know the community is not going to let Bigger go. Buckley cries, "Your
Honor, in the name of Almighty God, I plead with you to
be merciful to us!" He is facing an inescapable fact: to say
that we may have "made" Bigger what he is, that may be
true. But the damage has been done. It has been accumulat-
ing and maiming for centuries. But what are the people in
that room, facing that Bigger, supposed to do about it? They
face a boy who killed twice in twenty-four hours, killed
black and white. It becomes a question for the reader. Given
the fact that the society into which Bigger would ultimately
re-enter is not going to be changed, and given the present
sad state of psychiatric tools to rehabilitate him wholly,
what is to be done? Perhaps the most humane course, though
it is a wretched one, is to allow him to live out his life in
prison. And this is what Boris Max asks.

But that isn't what *Native Son* is all about. Again the
courtroom scene only distracts us from Wright's central
vision. Max says, "In a certain sense, every Negro in America's on trial out there today." But that "certain sense" is
terribly important, and here in part three of his novel
Wright has it wrong.

He said in "How Bigger Was Born" that "what Bigger
meant had claimed me because I felt with all of my being
that he was more important than what any person, white or

black, would say or try to make of him, more important
than any political analysis designed to explain or deny
him, more important even, than my own sense of fear, shame,
and diffidence." But "what Bigger meant" had not sufficiently "claimed" him so that he could resist the impulse
to "try to make" an explanatory rhetoric that would "deny
him." Or, to be fully fair, Bigger had "claimed" Richard
Wright in the first two sections of the book to the point of
utter possession.

III

In *Black Skin, White Masks,* Frantz Fanon comments
briefly on the character of Bigger Thomas. Before the murder of Mary Dalton, Fanon says, "No one knows yet who
[Bigger] is, but he knows that fear will fill the world when
the world finds out. And when the world knows, the world
always expects something of the Negro. He is afraid lest the
world know, he is afraid of the fear that the world would
feel if the world knew." And so, "Bigger Thomas acts. To
put an end to his tension, he acts, he responds to the world's
anticipation." And in this sense, killing is not really something Bigger does; it is something he is. An undeniable part
of his personality, the act is his mind. All his life he can wait
for it to happen to him. Murder is his cultural reality. "He
had killed many times before," Wright says, "only on those
other times there had been no handy victim of circumstance
to make visible or dramatic his will to kill." In such a world,
the murder becomes as inescapable as the terms of a logical
proposition.

At the beginning of the story Bigger's mother cries out at
him, "We wouldn't have to live in this garbage dump if you
had any manhood in you." The kitchenette is an assault on
his manhood. The squalor is the sign of a submerged man-

liness, a masculinity so utterly choked off that it wastes away. The slum means every day to his ears and eyes and nose only one thing: White Power. Crazed with black impotence he awakes to find giant rats attacking his women. "He hated his family because he knew that they were suffering and that he was powerless to help them." The utter pity of his dangling the dead rat before the women's eyes is not just that he gets a kick out of scaring them; dangling the rat's body before their eyes he is offering some little proof of his power. See this, I killed it. I am *some*thing of a man. I can kill.

The scene with the rat establishes in the opening pages the dimensions of the curse and provides for Bigger's murders as a psychic and cultural inevitability. It is not just that the white folks live somewhere on a green hill; when Gus asks Bigger where they live Bigger doubles his fist and strikes his solar plexus: "Right down here in my stomach." To kill the whites is a way, the only way, for Bigger to take "fully upon himself the crime of being black." The two crimes are logical consequences of each other.

Stephen Marcus has written that "one of the principal components in male sexuality is the desire for power, the desire to dominate. In modern society, money is one of the two or three most important instruments of personal power, and the association of sex and money through the medium of power is an inevitable one." It is inevitable for Bigger Thomas: famished in his desire to dominate, frustrated of any means for that domination, his triumph is to "settle at last" the old score through rape and ransom, a violation of the beautiful money-princess in the white castle. That is his only power, bringing the violence home, to invent horror in the horror that invented him. It is his inevitable vocation. Erik Erikson suggests in *Young Man Luther* that "probably the most neglected problem in psychoanalysis is the problem of work. . . . Decades of case histories have omitted the work histories of patients or have treated their occupation as a seemingly irrelevant area of life," and yet "many a delinquency begins by society's denial of the one gift on which a destructive individual's precarious identity depends." Which is exactly the point with Bigger: his power has nowhere to go. The problem is a central one in psychoanalytic study—the way work structures the psyche. For Freud, the individual's relationship to work does not just involve economic security but also the achievement of psychic equilibrium. The question, Who am I? in a capitalistic "democracy" involves and is intimately a part of the question, What do I do? And Bigger cannot *be,* in any constructive way, because the culture in which he lives will not let him *do*—do anything more than stand on street corners. Bigger drifts. He waits. His mind drifts and waits. He moves only in violent fantasies, with nothing other than dreams of destruction to give himself to. Wherever his aggressiveness turns, it is stopped up. His remark on the street corner— "Them white boys sure can fly"—is a literal truth, an axiom; the whites surely can fly and Bigger cannot. He is acknowledging not only their skill but his inability ever to have the chance of attaining it. When Max asks him in the cell what he wanted to be, every desire is one of escape, power, integration of mind and muscle. But it is a Jim Crow army, a navy where blacks wash dishes. Everything in his world equips Bigger to be a soldier of enormous effectiveness. In that sense he is a most useful commodity for the society. He can do its killing. But the culture denies him that "pleasure."

The continuing image of his dilemma is in a sensation of impotence, of falling. Gus says with "uneasy eagerness" to Bigger's premonition that "something going to happen to me . . . something I can't help . . ." that "It's like you going to fall." What Bigger and Gus speak on the street

corner comes true in the Dalton bedroom, where the something Bigger can't help is thrust upon him and he feels "as
though he were falling from a great height in a dream." It is
a dream that tortures him in his last time with Bessie when,
as he enters her, "the wind became so strong that it lifted
him high into the dark air, turning him, twisting him,
hurling him . . . at a moment he could not remember, he
had fallen. . . ." And when he plays black soldier on the
street he cries not just for destruction of the whites but a
special destruction—"Look ut the white folks *fall*" (my emphasis). When he escapes from the Dalton house he hurtles
through the window and falls, urinating, in the snow. And
when white society captures him on the rooftops, "his body
teetered on the edge . . . then he was falling." The white
world's phallic power ruins and rips his out; he is finally
captured when he is thrown into the air by a burst from the
white "hose" that ejects him from his frozen bed.

Bigger is a Native Son. Jean Paul Sartre has written that
racist oppression produces "neither man nor animal" but
"the native." Wright's title means more than that he is just
American; it means more carefully than that, and means
America's possession of him is a special one. For Bigger
Thomas to come fully into his title, he must be truly
"native" to the land that tells him he must kill. Fanon says
in *The Wretched of the Earth* that "the native is an op-
pressed person whose permanent dream is to become the
persecutor" and "the native who decides to put the pro-
gramme into practice, and to become its moving force, is
ready for violence at all times. From birth it is clear to him
that this narrow world, strewn with prohibitions, can only
be called in question by absolute violence."

It is that perception which redeems the final pages of
Native Son, where Wright makes a partial recovery from the
disasters of the courtroom. Bigger, as a national child, has
gone out in the course of the story to seek his manhood.

We are the most violent of nations, the country that has found the way to destroy the best. Our heroes traditionally are men of great violence, our Jesse Jameses, and John Dillingers, and Al Capones. Someone once said that our western heroes had to ride white horses because if they didn't, we could not tell them from the bad guys. Native Son is America's child by entering into her murders. If murder is freedom, it is because Bigger is entering into the cliché and living most fully exactly that role white society places upon the Negro. He is the black man's Horatio Alger, the good little bad boy who has a dream and works it out. He is our black Poor Richard, our black Gatsby, and his life is a success story. His greatest success must be a great horror for he finally comes to embody all the junk of the nightmare. It is not a contradiction to call him a "beast of the skull" (a phantom) and to call him also a boy on the ghetto streets, for he is a walking, breathing nightmare, the social fact in its purest form. If a culture works hard enough on the assumption that the black man is a dirty nigger, it is inevitable that a culture of such enormous power will turn some black men into dirty niggers. The final success is to make the myth prowl the streets.

Bigger has heard what the white world will do with him. He has heard Buckley in the courtroom. Fanon has pointed out that the master, the racist colonizer, always refers to his subject in zoological terms. Buckley's courtroom speech is a protracted bestiary, jerking in sadism:

Every decent white man in America ought to swoon with joy for the opportunity to crush with his heel the woolly black head of this black lizard, to keep him from scuttling on his belly farther over the earth and spitting forth his venom of death!

And Bigger, too, "swoons with joy" when he is able to mutilate the white head. At the very end of the book Big-

ger shouts that he didn't want to kill. "But what I killed
for, I *am!* It must've been pretty deep in me to make me
kill!" The ideological spokesman retreats, pleading "desperately," and his eyes are "full of terror." Only young Jan
Erlone had been able to convince Bigger of real understanding. (And Jan Erlone is modeled on Wright's real-life
friend, Jan Wittenber. "Erlone" is Wright's dialect tribute
that, as he said, Jan *alone* among the white comrades was
capable of real sympathy.) But at the end of the novel Boris
Max can only filter Bigger through the Party's vision. Max
can explain Bigger to the white courtroom; alone with Bigger, Max is lost. He murmurs, "no; no; no . . . Bigger, not
that. . . ." Bigger, finally, is black all the time.

The agony for Wright at the end of the book is the terror
of his terms. The black boy ends up as he began, caged.
Wright had opened the door in the forensics of the courtroom, but even that could not pull the beast out. At the end
Bigger is simply there—like *The Hairy Ape* in the last scene
of O'Neill's play—and in spite of all the ideas Wright has
brought forward to retrieve him, Bigger "smiled a faint, wry,
bitter smile." Whenever he had thought of murder he
"smiled"; after he murdered he "smiled"; and now that
smile is all of it, the final excruciating expression of his life.

The achievement of the novel is an understanding of this
hate, not an exaltation of it. What is meant by saying that if
one lives too long with the beast one can love it is that the
mark of one's authenticity becomes the virulence of one's
rage. The only "real" Negro is "black crazy." Throughout
the novel we are in there with Bigger, feeling in unbearable
physical terms the massiveness of his hate. Facing the private
detective, Bigger "hated Britten so hard and hot, while
standing there with sleepy eyes and parted lips . . . for a
split second a roaring noise in his ears blotted out sound."
The physical terms are unbearable: he is deafened by his

hate and yet he must stand as a colored boy "with sleepy eyes and parted lips"—a hate that cannot be let out in a striking lash, a hate that grows even more unbearable by the absolute necessity of being what the white man expects. Throughout the novel we are continually facing such moments with Bigger, participating with him as he endures them. But we should be rather more accurate than several critics have been in defining our relationship to that feeling. We do not "sympathize" with Bigger. We *feel with* him, perhaps, but we do it in a special way. When Fanon speaks of violence, and the necessity for it, he addresses himself to a revolutionary social situation. "Violence" is impelled by consciousness. The hatred of "the native" is at the service of an idea and his destruction is a necessary prelude to a social creation. Violence is not a helpless reflex, a gross futility, an insane outburst. It is part of the large, communal act: repossession of the African home. But the violent blood baths of Bigger Thomas are at the mercy of the system which engendered them. He hacks his way to a dead end.

Bigger had nothing other than his hate, nowhere to go with it. And America electrocutes her native son when he claims his birthright in the fullness of paralyzing rage.

CHAPTER 5

An American Life

When Richard Wright realized the final
meaning of Bigger Thomas he saw there
was no place to go. He was facing a wall.
So, as he had done so often in his life when
he faced a wall, he went straight ahead. To
Black Boy. The book had begun as "The
Ethics of Living Jim Crow," the essay
Wright prepared for the anthology of the
Federal Writers' Project; now he was ready
to keep all the promises in the "Ethics" and
explore larger questions. There were other,
exciting projects in the five-year interval
between *Native Son* and *Black Boy*—his
text for the photo-collection of *12 Million
Black Voices,* stories to write, reviews to get
in, speeches to deliver—but his autobiography was slowly taking shape in his mind.

Native Son is a story of the North, of the

city, where enraged violence expresses itself in overt assault. Bigger is just coming into his manhood, into the full terms of the curse which corrodes his brain and leads him to kill. *Black Boy* is a Southern story, a story of the country; a boy who must painfully, gradually learn the curse, who totters beneath the blows he receives. The books go together, novel and autobiography, fiction and fact, the twin peaks of Richard Wright's career. Both take us into the mind of a single black boy in America, one destroyed by crippling hate and the other making an uncanny survival.

Wright's effort in *Black Boy* would not be to exorcise another version of "the bad nigger" that was living in his skull; here he would inspect all his own old scars, make them open wounds again, assess the pain and try to heal. Proust could symbolize his ideal ecstasy in the moment when *Maman* kissed him good night each evening, sealing the warm world of total pleasure; in this black boy's remembrance of things past the mother beats her son into unconsciousness. Daily terror leads to feverish dreams of Granny's sick flaming hair and "huge wobbly white bags, like the full udders of cows, suspended from the ceiling above me" and goggled-eyed kittens hanging by the neck, spitting in air, ready to claw his eyes. In *Black Boy* Wright would re-enter the haunted house of his youth, and summon the gross spirits to intelligence.

Black Boy clarifies the nature of Wright's importance. In any strictly literary sense, he broke no new ground, established no new devices or techniques or methods. He did not make us see our experience in new ways; he made us see new experience. He had a perception about America, a perception of a part of America that was unknown territory. His importance is not really literary but what we should call cultural. We come to him not for new ways of saying things but for the new things he has to say. When he does get

"literary" on us, when he draws himself up into "writing,"
he is merely fancy, and he fails. He would say of his effort in
Black Boy, "If I could fasten the mind of the reader upon
words so firmly that he would forget words and be conscious
only of his response, I felt that I would be in sight of knowing how to write narrative. I strove to master words, to make
them disappear. . . ." His ability to do that is a major
achievement of *Black Boy*, a book virtually uncontaminated
by his old rhetoric. In *Native Son* there was too much
forensic slag, too many set pieces, a prose racing in all directions, and an explanatory moral. Five years later, Wright
has freed himself of his revolutionary slogans and all that
went with them; he has grown into his craft and his sense
of his life's meaning.

The book is extremely difficult to describe. The power of
the prose is explainable largely by its effect. Wright wanted
the words, as he said, to disappear. He had to set the facts
down in front of us, carefully in clear light, and then we
would see. When we do see, what more is there to say?
Surely no one needs to "interpret" what we perceive when
young Richard, famished for books, gets the permission of a
white Irish Catholic, a "Pope lover . . . hated by the white
Southerners" to forge his name on a note to the white
librarian in Memphis (where black people were forbidden
to patronize the shelves): *"Dear Madam: Will you please let
this nigger boy have some books by H. L. Mencken?"* One of
Wright's wisest choices was not to "interpret" that encounter—what should he say that we cannot see?—and one of
his finest achievements was to make a note that embodied
the situation.

Although Lillian Smith's review of *Black Boy* in *PM* was
generally quite favorable, she complained:

His childhood is still, in large part, a closed door to him.
He has not yet found the key that will unlock old memories and

bring back deeply buried childhood feeling. He tells little incidents, little, heart-breaking, pitiful, and sometimes amusing anecdotes. But they are told with a strange lack-of-feeling tone, with little of that quality of imagination that interprets even as it narrates. . . .

Exactly the opposite is true: that "strange lack-of-feeling tone" (whatever it means) may be Miss Smith's way of objecting to the starkness, the unrelieved pain. All life is perceived here in such brutal and corrosive terms that to interpret the details or events would be to draw us away from Wright's accuracy, to swamp his sharp, swift craft with baggy yards of sail. Wright's refusal to provide what Lillian Smith asks for is his dignity as a writer and contributes to the difficult integrity of his book. The story is too important for us to weep over, and the implications of that story cannot be adequately understood if we have been lulled into tears.

Black Boy is, as the subtitle says, "A Record of Childhood and Youth." Here we will not find the unbearable fantasies of the culture, which Wright had previously embodied in Bigger Thomas. In Native Son we were shown almost nothing of Bigger's background; while his early life may have been no great mystery to us, it did not exist in any detail. The facts about him, before that dreadful winter day, were sketched in only as answers to Jan's questions in Ernie's Kitchen Shack. Bigger says he was born in Mississippi, quit school at the eighth grade, had been in Chicago five years, and his father had been killed long ago in a riot in the South. In Black Boy we can see Richard Wright's similarity to Bigger: born in Mississippi, a formal schooling that ended at the eighth grade, bereft of his father at an early age, and going north to Chicago at the end of his adolescence.

But Richard Wright did not become Bigger Thomas; he created him. If Black Boy can be made to fill in all Bigger's blanks, it also raises another significant question: how did it happen that Richard escaped? Malcolm X wrote near the end of his autobiography:

I feel, and I hope, that if I honestly and fully tell my life's account, read objectively it might prove to be a testimony of some social value.

I think that an objective reader may see how in the society to which I was exposed as a black youth here in America, for me to wind up in a prison was really just about inevitable.

Wright, too, is presenting "honestly and fully" his "life's account" and he is obviously intending it "to be a testimony of some social value." In Bigger's story Wright had shown that when the "black youth" ended up in an electric chair it was "really just about inevitable." In *Black Boy* he was showing how all the horror could make a Bigger, how the whole black society was ripped up and torn apart by that horror, but he was also showing how he himself escaped it.

Most of it was sheer luck. That saves the book from any hint of mere strutting; we see over and over again that when Richard pulled out of a beating, or escaped a fire, or didn't get a bullet in his brain—all those survivals had little to do with his own power or his own brains. When he wins a fight, he wins it out of utter desperation, backed against a wall fighting for his life; his tormentors lay off because they don't want to get hurt (one of those wild blows might, after all, land), but they're not afraid of getting beaten. If Richard had only wised up, he would have been saved innumerable beatings at home, countless disgraces by the white men. His survival is no puffing pride at his own cunning or strength; too often we see him duped and flat on his back.

But his survival is not only luck, and what else it was involves considerable moral force. *Black Boy* was Wright's second enormous best seller, and when he wrote to Gertrude Stein on May 27, 1945, he could bring the news that again a book of his had been out only a few months and the sales were in the hundreds of thousands. To explain his success he confesses, "Frankly, I don't know why people read my work; it upsets them terribly. . . ." But we should get upset in the right way, and Wright knew it more clearly than his flip "frankly I don't know why people read my work" might imply. It was absolutely remarkable that the pickaninny he describes could grow up to be a writer; on all sides people were constantly turning him from that goal, shaming him out of it, laughing him out of it, beating him out of it. From the beginning his "Granny" had "always burned the books I had brought into the house, branding them as worldly." When at the end he looked back, he saw that his dream of being a writer was one "which the entire educational system of the South had been rigged to stifle." That he should be able to live to tell the tale was a freak of determination.

It is also central to our sense of what the "record" means. When Lionel Trilling reviewed *Black Boy* in the *Nation* (April 7, 1945), he said that here was "a remarkably fine book," but its fineness could not be understood merely by those who saw it as another report of misery and oppression. We had several of those books, and too many readers had enjoyed them cheaply:

> To sit in one's armchair and be harrowed can all too easily pass for a moral or political action. We vicariously suffer in slippers and become virtuous; it is pleasant to exercise moral indignation at small cost; or to fill up emotional vacancy with good strong feeling at a safe distance; or to feel consciously superior to the brutal oppressor; or to be morally entertained by poverty. . . .

Trilling felt that Wright did not allow us those luxuries. In *Black Boy* Wright "does not wholly identify himself with his painful experience, does not, therefore, make himself a mere object of the reader's consciousness, does not make

himself that different kind of human being, a 'sufferer.' He
is not an object; he is a subject. . . ."

At the Memphis bank young Richard got to know a
"round, yellow, fat elevator operator" named Shorty. He
was "the most amazing specimen of the southern Negro I
had ever met" not only because of his grotesque appearance
("the complexion of a Chinese, a short forehead, and three
chins"), but also because this "hardheaded, sensible reader
of magazines and books . . . proud of his race and in-
dignant about its wrongs" would "play the role of a clown
of the most debased and degraded type" whenever white
folks were around. One day Shorty needed a quarter for
lunch; he told Richard he would get it from the first white
man who came by. When one walked in, Shorty went into
his act, begging, then refusing to run the elevator, "drooling,
drawling, grimacing, clowning." And finally he gets the
white man to ask what he'd do for a quarter. Shorty—
giggling all the while—bent down, "poked out his broad,
fleshy ass" and offered it to be kicked. For two bits.

The white man laughed softly, jingled some coins in his
pocket, took out one and thumped it to the floor. Shorty stooped
to pick it up and the white man bared his teeth and swung his
foot into Shorty's rump with all the strength of his body.
Shorty let out a howling laugh that echoed up and down the
elevator shaft.

After Shorty's laugh—"This monkey's got the peanuts"—
young Richard goes up to him with "only disgust and
loathing" and asks, "How in God's name can you do that?"

"Listen, nigger," he said to me, "my ass is tough and
quarters is scarce."

Richard Wright despised that man. In *Black Boy* young
Richard always clings to his dignity, even in moments of
great suffering, even when that precarious dignity of his gets
another white boot in the ass. Shorty is partially redeemed

by his humor, by his gross indifference to the sanctity of
his rear end. He is redeemed, too, by the fact that he has
made his ass tough enough to trust it, and he does inhabit
a world where quarters are extremely scarce. But Richard
Wright had none of Shorty's capacity for buffoonery and he
set a higher price on his person. Over two decades later,
Eldridge Cleaver would take a similar stand, quoting a
central article of faith from Norman Mailer: "Being a man
is the continuing battle of one's life, and one loses a bit of
manhood with every stale compromise to the authority of
any power in which one does not believe." And that is the
continuing cry in all the battles of Black Boy's life: No
compromise.

In Arthur Miller's The Crucible, a frosty Salem elder is
accused of witchery. The old man will not give in. To get
the admission out of him the judges pile stone after stone
upon his chest. As he dies, he utters only two words, "More
weight."

"More weight" is adequate to the horror and to the moral
splendor of Black Boy. Young Richard is an object of a mass
aberration, a witch-hunt in which he is a little black devil.
The community keeps piling the crushing circumstances
upon him. As he grows he grows to an awareness of just
how heavy are the things pressing down on him, begins to
see just how hard the white world has to crush. He refuses
to give in. No matter how much "more weight" the culture
heaps upon him, he will not die into the lowly "nigger" that
they want him to be. And when he finally escapes that
system, there is a subsequent determination in the writing
not to tidy the ordeal with facile pathos. Given all his luck,
all his dignity, and all his will, it was unlikely that the boy
would survive. But if he did, he could tell us just how much
energy had been expended on both sides of the rocks, the
world that pressed them down and the small voice that called

up from below. Some reviewers objected that Wright's book only showed that the system could not have been as bad as he said—his survival proved, that is, his survival. What it does prove is that all the rocks had not yet killed all the black boys. One that got away was able to tell us why they had not—and how close they had come. He told us in such a way that if we chose to shed our tears we would have to see that they only watered the rocks.

I I

The book opens with the house burning down. Richard was bored, it was winter night, and all the attention went elsewhere; he could not play outside and he could not make noise inside because "in the next room Granny lay ill." The scene sets the pitch for the book as a whole: throughout, someone is in deep trouble, wasting away, sick, in the immediate vicinity of a new and even ghastlier trouble. Out of boredom and sickness, a fire. Everywhere in the book Wright is showing us how the ennui, the varieties of illness, and the explosions are hopelessly linked together in an unending and unbreakable circle of oppression.

Richard's "first triumph over my father" is the desperate victory of a false literalness. The kitten outside disturbs the father's sleep and so he yells, "Get rid of it, kill it." Richard, thirsting for excitement and desperate to prove his own power in the world, strings the kitten up. The way to vent all one's bottled-up hate (and not get whipped for it) is to take exasperations as imperatives. But if the father will not whip, the mother will.

His first school is an outdoor privy. He learns to identify his neighbors by their backsides, to gauge their determination by the "projectile force of their excretions." Knowledge begins at the back end of an open-end commode; the course is the law of bodily functions. And this school will be in every school he attends, schools of endurance and dirt. Unable to escape a paralysis at the blackboard, he comes away with all the schoolyard graffiti, spreading it in soap on the neighborhood windows. And when Fundamentalist Granny scrubs his backside in the bath,

My mind was in a sort of daze, midway between daydreaming and thinking. Then, before I knew it, words—words whose meaning I did not fully know—had slipped out of my mouth.
"When you get through, kiss back there."

As usual, he has learned too much of the wrong thing. Granny says he has done "something he ought to be killed for." After his beating he is told that he has been whipped for learning "foul practices" and "when I asked what 'foul practices' were, my mother beat me afresh." His schooling takes place in the toilet; he is beaten on the way in and on the way out.

He has nothing to hold him together, to keep him whole. _Black Boy_ is a portrait of unending hunger. When his father won't provide food, Richard hates him with a "biological bitterness." Each night he sees "hunger standing at my bedside, staring at me." Later, at the foster home, when he has to mow the lawn by pulling up the grass in his hands, "I was too weak from hunger . . . I would grow dizzy and my mind would become blank and I would find myself, after an interval of unconsciousness, upon my hands and knees, my head whirling, my eyes staring in bleak astonishment at the green grass. . . ." Wherever we enter the narrative, we can read hardly a page before we see again the intolerable effects of not having enough to eat. At Uncle Hoskins's house, he is told that he should "get used to food," but every time he leaves the table he has to steal a little bread for his pockets. "In washing my clothes my mother found the

gummy wads and scolded me to break me of the habit; I
stopped hiding the bread in my pockets and hid it about the
house, in corners, behind dressers." And he was right to store
it away for very soon Uncle Hoskins gets killed by whites.
He "had simply been plucked from our midst"—and the
ordeal of hunger is on again. At Granny's house they rarely
have any meat. "For breakfast I ate mush and gravy made
from flour and lard and for hours afterwards I would belch
it up into my mouth." He concludes that his diet "would
have stunted an average-sized dog." His pride will not allow
him to get the little food that is available from others; in
the playground with the other kids, "whenever they asked
me if I wanted food, I would say no, even though I was
starving." And one of the quietest moments in the book is
the end of chapter two where his single Christmas gift is an
orange. He eats it all day long, and at night, just before
going to bed, "I tore the peeling into bits and munched
them slowly."

Hunger is the most important thing in his life; over the
years we continue to see how "hunger would make me weak,
would make me sway while walking." But the hunger in his
belly is only the most numbing physical pang of a general
hunger. Midway through the book, "I vowed that someday
I would end this hunger of mine, this apartness, this eternal
difference." Hunger is wanting to have, to eat, to be filled.

Except for one brief paragraph about the boy's infatua-
tion with the Reverend's wife in the choir, there is no sexual
love in *Black Boy*—not even puppy love. When he tries to
find out about sex he peeks into a whore house, falls from
the window, and the madam comes out to scold. "Evidently
I had done something terrible"—as usual. Years later as a
bellboy he looks at a naked white prostitute strutting in
front of him, and a white man says, "Keep your eyes where
they belong if you want to be healthy!" When in Memphis

a simple little black girl offers herself to him, wants to marry and love him and comb his hair, he asks himself, "Was I dumb or was she dumb?" For so many years Richard had been looking for love, any love he could get; on the couch in the prim little home "the light that shone out of this child's heart . . . blinded me."

The year after *Black Boy* appeared Wright did an article for *Twice a Year* in which he said (the italics are his):

At the core of the personality of almost every delinquent child is found *emotional deprivation,* and this exists in a land where Negroes are traditionally regarded as possessing, as a gift of nature, a super-abundant fund of laughter, song, joy, and rhythm.

The sadness Richard Wright felt in Memphis in 1925, when Mrs. Moss thrust her simple little Bess on him, was that here he could see for the first time "the full degree to which my life at home had cut me off, not only from white people but from Negroes as well." The hunger had not been satisfied anywhere; it had stunted his growth. "My personality was lopsided." Hit too many times, "I felt that I had been slapped out of the human race." The whites would never take him in and the blacks had thrown him out. The price for standing up to his Uncle Tom had been even greater than he had thought it would be, for Uncle Tom kept all children away from him: "No matter how carefully I weighed my memories, I could recall no innocent intimacy, no games, no playing, none of the association that usually exists between young people living in the same house." The behavior of Uncle Tom and the other elders illustrates what Erik Erikson has said in *Young Man Luther*: "The most deadly of all possible sins is the mutilation of a child's spirit; for such mutilation undercuts the life principle of trust. . . ."

Young Richard turned to the only thing that he had to trust. Books. Words. As money "melted into the bottomless hunger of the household" Richard "hungered for a different life." As he entered seventh grade, "my old hunger was still with me, and I lived on what I did not eat." Perhaps in books, in stories, he could find some food.

He is the only one in the community with that kind of hunger, and such a portrait could be violently misunderstood. *Time*'s reviewer (March 5, 1945) said that *Black Boy* was "the story of a man set apart from his own race by sensitivity and intellect, yet barred forever from the white race by the color of his skin." The assumption in the sentence, of course, is that poor Richard's "sensitivity and intellect" separate him "from his own race" because that race is incapable of the "sensitivity and intellect" which only whites can have. Richard, your whole trouble is that while on the outside you are black, inside you're really white like us. And when such white readers looked through the pages of *Black Boy* for portraits of "sensitive" or "intellectual" Negroes they would find only Richard. If Wright could say that the whites always thought of the blacks as "a variety of children," he did not provide much evidence for thinking the opposite. He seemed to join in, to accept the prejudice, saying:

Our anger was like the anger of children, passing quickly from one petty grievance to another, from the memory of one slight wrong to another.

To say such things—and to show them over and over again in the portraits he drew of his family—opened Wright to charges not only from the unserious white reader but also from several black readers. Again he was facing the problem of *Native Son,* and facing it even more dangerously, for this was supposed to be fact, not fiction.

The virulent attack by W. E. B. Du Bois in the New York *Herald Tribune* (March 4, 1945) was formidable; here, after all, was another spokesman for the race. Du Bois's review is a curious document, and he seems unable to convince himself (or to admit to the reader) that the story is true. "The hero whom Wright draws, *and maybe it is himself,* is in his childhood a loathsome brat, foul-mouthed, and 'a drunkard'" (my emphasis). When Wright portrays the people around him he is not to be trusted because "the Negroes whom he paints have almost no redeeming qualities. Some work hard, some are sly, many are resentful; but there is none who is ambitious, successful, or really intelligent." Success, one gathers, is "a redeeming quality." Du Bois apparently felt that such a book could do nothing but damage, portraying to a mass white audience a picture of the Negro as a depraved being. It would confirm the prejudices that Du Bois himself had so long been working to tear down.

The most fiery objection would come many years later in an attack that far excels that of Du Bois in its appearance of elegance and its cultivated weariness of false definitions. When *Black Boy* first appeared Ralph Ellison praised it in "Richard Wright's Blues" for *Antioch Review* (June 1945). Ellison found the best things, the "fresh, human responses" in those passages that are probably the worst things in the book, the corn-pone lists of natural beauties that Wright felt compelled to put in here and there. These sections, which Ellison admired, could be written for high-school "voice of democracy" contests, colorless Americana.

> There was the breathlessly anxious fun of chasing and catching flitting fireflies on drowsy summer nights.
> There was the drenching hospitality in the pervading smell of sweet magnolias.
> There was the aura of limitless freedom distilled from the rolling sweep of tall green grass swaying and glinting in the wind and sun.

There was the feeling of impersonal plenty when I saw a boll of cotton whose cup had split over and straggled its white fleece toward the earth.

There was the pitying chuckle that bubbled in my throat when I watched a fat duck waddle across the back yard.

And so on. Wright has four of these little lists, and they add nothing to the book. One can hear them recited breathlessly into the microphone by Miss Alabama: "And somewhere in the back of my mind—" she wiggles in her swimsuit—"a voice whispered: *America*." But this is what Ellison liked, at the time, and when his own taste became a little more secure he got on to more complicated errors. What so appalled him in this "Record of Childhood and Youth" was the conclusion Wright had drawn from his portraits of viciousness and destitution. In *Shadow and Act* Ellison quotes and then attacks a passage at the beginning of chapter two in *Black Boy*. Wright said that

I used to mull over the strange absence of real kindness in Negroes, how unstable was our tenderness, how lacking in genuine passion we were, how void of great hope, how timid our joy, how bare our traditions, how hollow our memories, how lacking we were in those intangible sentiments that bind man to man, and how shallow was even our despair. After I had learned other ways of life I used to brood upon the unconscious irony of those who felt that Negroes led so passional an existence! I saw that what had been taken for our emotional strength was our negative confusions, our flights, our fears, our frenzy under pressure.

Ellison was moved to his essay partly by Irving Howe's estimate of Wright's importance in "Black Boys and Native Sons" (in which Howe had said that Ellison was "literary to a fault"). Ellison responded that just as "How Bigger Was Born" had been Wright's

Jamesian preface to *Native Son*, the passage quoted above is his paraphrase of Henry James' catalogue of those items of a high civilization which were absent from American life during Hawthorne's day, and which seemed so necessary in order for the novelist to function. This, then, was Wright's list of those items of high humanity which he found missing among Negroes. Thank God, I have never been quite that literary.

Wright, said Ellison, was free to present himself as a hunger-crazed child, desperate for values, but he should have had the grace and the sense not to project his troubles onto his people, and certainly not to do it in the name of literature.

But this is surely being "literary" on Ellison's part. The passage in *Black Boy* is by no stretch of the imagination comparable to James's list; that Ellison could think so (or say so, as a way of getting back at Howe) is a sign of his deep uneasiness. Wright was saying that in the terrible cultural bind of the South, the Negro's pain and desire to get out of that violence was all bottled up, constantly turning on other Negroes. In *Native Son* Bigger and his gang "had always robbed Negroes. They felt that it was much easier and safer to rob their own people, for they knew that white police-men never really searched diligently for Negroes who committed crimes against other Negroes." And in *Black Boy* young Richard "had seen many Negroes solve the problem of being black by transferring their hatred of themselves to others with a black skin and fighting them." He and his friend, Harrison, know they have been tricked into fighting each other so that the white men could enjoy it for sport: "The shame and anger we felt for having allowed ourselves to be duped crept into our blows and blood ran into our eyes, half blinding us. The hate we felt for the men whom we had tried to cheat went into the blows we threw at each other."

But that is only part of Wright's point in his passage on why the Negroes he knew in the South lacked what Ellison calls "high humanity." In *Black Boy* Wright was trying to find a meaning in the unrelieved horror and shame. Ellison takes the passage out of context, ignoring the various ways Wright is trying to show us how this gross state came about. He refuses to dress up his Negroes in an imported Sunday best because he has a far larger task before him and he is far too seriously engaged to fall into the old error that if you write about the Negro, put him on stage or in a movie, he must always wear a coat and tie.

Wright's reflections on the Negro are crucially placed in *Black Boy*. Beginning chapter two, they follow the portrait of Wright's father which concluded chapter one. Wright had met his father for what was to be the last time, on Wright's return from his trip to Mexico in 1940. A quarter of a century had gone by now, since the father had run out on the family, and Wright's discovery of what the years had done to his father, and to himself, produced one of the very finest vignettes he would ever be able to do, a portrait that is almost unbearable in its sense of distance and waste and loss. The son confronts the ruin of his father "standing alone upon the red clay of a Mississippi plantation, a share-cropper, clad in ragged overalls, holding a muddy hoe in his gnarled, veined hands." Here Wright's prose is working at its very best: all the details are sharply done, there are no superfluous ones, and the language is almost entirely free of false phrases or unnecessary moralizing.

When I tried to talk to him I realized that, though ties of blood made us kin, though I could see a shadow of my face in his face, though there was an echo of my voice in his voice, we were forever strangers, speaking a different language, living on vastly different planes of reality. That day a quarter of a century later when I visited him on the plantation—he was standing against the sky, smiling toothlessly, his hair whitened, his body bent, his eyes glazed with dim recollection, his fearsome aspect of twenty-five years ago gone forever from him—I was over-whelmed to realize that he could never understand me or the scalding experiences that had swept me beyond his life and into an area of living that he could never know. I stood before him, poised, my mind aching as it embraced the simple naked-ness of his life, feeling how completely his soul was imprisoned by the slow flow of the seasons, by wind and rain and sun, how fastened were his memories to a crude and raw past, how chained were his actions and emotions to the direct, animalistic impulses of his withering body. . . .

From the white landowners above him there had not been handed to him a chance to learn the meaning of loyalty, of sentiment, of tradition. Joy was as unknown to him as was despair. As a creature of the earth, he endured, hearty, whole, seemingly indestructible, with no regrets and no hope. He asked easy, drawling questions about me, his other son, his wife, and he laughed, amused, when I informed him of their destinies.

The confrontation of these two men on the red Mississippi dirt is one which must have involved Wright in a great agony, for he was calling across irretrievable time to his father—the father that in *Black Boy* he associates with his dizzying hunger. They stand apart, talking softly, the son and the "endured, hearty, whole, seemingly indestructible" father whose whole life had been destruction—the "black peasant who had gone to the city seeking life, but who had failed in the city; a black peasant whose life had been hope-lessly snarled in the city, and who had at last fled the city." And it is from the deep sadness of that encounter that Wright goes on to his list of what Negroes seemed to him to lack, how it all had been torn from them.

To say that Wright's passage is "Jamesian" is absurd. Wright is attempting to find the meaning he has presented in that horrid distance he felt from his father, trying to see why he could never have his father and his father never could fully have himself.

Wright continued his passage on the "absence" of re-deeming culture in Negro life by saying that

Whenever I thought of the essential bleakness of black life in America, I knew that Negroes had never been allowed to catch the full spirit of Western civilization, that they lived somehow in it but not of it. And when I brooded upon the cultural barrenness of black life, I wondered if clean, positive tenderness, love, honor, loyalty, and the capacity to remember were native with man. I asked myself if these human qualities were not fostered, won, struggled and suffered for, preserved in ritual from one generation to another.

Wright's portraits of unbearable physical damage are in themselves terrifying, but they are also part of unbearable psychic damage. He is showing us that racism does not only oppress bodily; it is more fully corrosive, more fully damaging. Southern superstition maims the mind, stunts it, inhibits tenderness, never encourages the "human qualities" that must be fostered if they are to survive. To say otherwise would be essentially unserious, intellectually and morally.

Wright chose as the epigraph for his work a passage from the Book of Job: "They meet with darkness in the daytime, And they grope at noonday as in the night." The burden of *Black Boy* is to show how the blindness of the communities, black and white, came about. After the elder brother of one of his chums had been shot, Richard sat on the front porch, brooding in "a temporary paralysis of will and impulse." He thought of the white world as "something whose horror and blood might descend upon me at any moment" and he was "compelled to give my entire imagination over to it, an act which blocked the springs of thought and feeling in me." The extraordinary power and ferocity of the white world does not allow the Negro community any sense of freedom for the rituals of communal life, does not allow men and women to acknowledge their humanity by all those ceremonies through which one learns, acquires, and continues responses that give us any liberating sense of ourselves.

When Uncle Hoskins is killed, "fear drowned out grief."
And, Wright shows us, if people are never given time for
grief, they will be unlikely to grieve. Hoskins was dead, but
"there was no funeral. There was no music. There was no
period of mourning. There were no flowers." None of those
tokens with which a culture makes peace with its dead are
allowed—there is too much danger that the white man will
"kill all his kinfolks!" The fact was that "Uncle Hoskins had
simply been plucked from our midst and we, figuratively,
had fallen on our faces to avoid looking into that white-hot
face of terror that we knew loomed somewhere above us."
Terror produces terror, brutality goes on into brutality.
When young Richard tries to "understand" what it all
means and why the black community had not fought back,
"I asked my mother, and the fear that was in her made her
slap me into silence." In such a world it is impossible to talk
about "culture" because the greatest energy in that world
makes culture unavailable, makes mother slap child re-
flexively.

Shocked, frightened, alone without their husbands or friends,
my mother and Aunt Maggie lost faith in themselves, and, after
much debate and hesitation, they decided to return home to
Granny and rest, think, map out new plans for living.

The phrases in the above sentence all carry a sharp charge,
for we realize that those words we use—"lost faith in themselves," "much debate and hesitation," "return home to
Granny," and the incredible sense of how utterly helpless
they are in "map out new plans for living"—all these figures
of speech are so utterly inadequate to the controlling emotion. This is *A Death in the Family* where the family has
nothing to do but run for its life.

Richard imitates the reflex where it does not apply.
Grandpa dies, not because whites have lynched him but

because he has finally reached the end of old age. When Richard is sent to Uncle Tom's house with the news, he behaves as if it were a repetition of the Uncle Hoskins incident, running "every inch of the two miles" and bounding up the steps and into the room where his uncle is sleeping. Richard runs to the bed, shakes his uncle awake:

"Uncle Tom, Granny says to come at once. Grandpa's dead."
He stared at me for a long time.
"You certainly are a prize fool," he said quietly. "Don't you know that that's no way to tell a person that his father's dead?"
I stared at him, baffled, panting.

Richard is "baffled" because he is only repeating the haste and frenzy of that other death he had seen. No "prize fool," he has only learned the lesson that the culture had taught him.

Wright knew and showed how "the culture of one black household was . . . transmitted to another black household, and folk tradition was handed from group to group." But he also saw how feeble that tradition was when the white world broke savagely in. He knew also how defective and how destructive any such "folk culture" would be in a land where those who exchanged it had no adequate education. In this sense Richard found himself to be one of the more fortunate children, for when he accompanied an insurance agent out onto the Delta plantation

I had been pitying myself for not having books to read, and now I saw children who had never read a book. Their chronic shyness made me seem bold and city-wise; a black mother would try to lure her brood into the room to shake hands with me and they would linger at the jamb of the door, peering at me with one eye, giggling hysterically.

And when in Memphis he told Mrs. Moss he was from Jackson she said, "You act mighty bright to be from there." She thought Jackson Negroes "just stand with their heads down, with one foot on top of the other and you have to guess at what they're trying to say."

Ignorant sickness infects the family's spiritual life: the oppressive brutalities of a Calvinist Christianity. When Richard first thought of bigotry in Memphis, he did not think of whites. "I discovered that all human beings were not mean and driving, were not bigots like the members of my family." His Granny and his Aunt Addie said "they were dead to the world, and those of their blood who lived in that world were therefore dead to them." And, of course, they *are* "dead" to the world, incapable of any lively, open response to it.

Granny and Aunt Addie quarreled and fought not only with me, but with each other over minor points of religious doctrine, or over some imagined infraction of what they chose to call their moral code. Wherever I found religion in my life I found strife, the attempt of one individual or group to rule another in the name of God.

In all of this Wright is gathering the material and providing the insights through which we can see the nature of the black community's disease. What the white man gives—and takes away—continually enslaves and thwarts the possibility that a black person can look toward anyone, white or black, with confidence.

Jean Paul Sartre wrote:

The order is given to reduce the inhabitants of the annexed country to the level of superior monkeys in order to justify the settler's treatment of them as beasts of burden. Violence in the colonies does not only have for its aim the keeping of these enslaved men at arm's length; it seeks to dehumanise them. Everything will be done to wipe out their traditions . . . and to destroy their culture without giving them ours. Sheer physical fatigue will stupefy them. Starved and ill, if they have any spirit left, fear will finish the job. . . .

Black Boy shows us this—the effect of having all culture wiped out, all paths to culture blockaded; Wright presents again and again the stupefying condition brought about not only in his own person but in those around him by the sheer physical fatigue as each day the family stumbles through the hours, starved, ill, numb. "I was already so conditioned toward my relatives that when I passed them I actually had a nervous tic in my muscles." All terror spins toward the center, and families fall apart twitching.

Yet an odd feature of those portraits is that so often they are etched in comedy. They are pathetic, endlessly hurt, but few in the family are merely passive—at least not passive when they have a Richard to intimidate; they loom up with ferocious energy into ghastly tragicomic figures of twisted power. Granny is one of Wright's greatest portraits and she inhabits a reality that we associate with a Dickensian grotesque. Just as Miss Havisham continually points her finger at Pip commanding, "Play" ("so that I may have the pleasure of observing"), so Granny continually points her finger at Richard commanding, "Sin" ("so that I may have the pleasure of beating the Hell out of you"). Granny is a Negro whose skin is white, a Christian who is continually sadistic. "Granny bore the standard for God, but she was always fighting." Wherever she turns she spreads destruction with a power that is entirely frightening! "Granny finally charged Ella with telling me things that I should not know and Ella, weeping and distraught, packed her things and moved." So utterly white is this black Granny that Richard enjoys going to town to watch the "baffled stares" of the whites who see one of their own color leading an "undeniably Negro" boy through the stores. Granny hurts herself by hitting too hard; her greatest discomfort comes when she lashes out at Richard, misses, and "the force of her blow was so strong that she fell down the steps, headlong, her aged body wedged in a narrow space between the fence and the bottom step." Grandpa has to tear the fence down to rescue her. We feel a certain clean joy when young Richard tells her, at the bath, to kiss his ass; it is an assault on her whole contorted world—this woman who seems incapable of kissing anything, incapable of admitting asses exist. When Richard tells her, she "seemed to have gone out of her mind," first becoming "terribly still" and then shrieking around the house for almighty vengeance.

Grandpa's voice is very quiet. He is in many ways Granny's opposite, her natural mate, as he quietly endures his own colossal illusion "that the war between the states would be resumed." Year in and year out he keeps "his Civil War rifle loaded in a corner" and his "blue uniform of the Union Army neatly folded." Grandpa is conspicuous by his silence, his hate all the more overpowering because it is inarticulate: "I never heard him speak of white people; I think he hated them too much to talk of them." And, as with Granny, Grandpa becomes a figure of grotesque comedy, unkillable delusion and will. He writes the War Department, asking for the back pay he will never get because the white officer who had signed him out was Swedish, recording "Richard Wilson" as "Richard Vinson." For decades Grandpa and Washington exchange letters that Grandpa cannot read or write but has to have someone else in the community take care of. His story is one of mighty exasperation and endurance:

He would name persons long dead, citing their ages and descriptions, reconstructing battles in which he had fought, naming towns, rivers, creeks, roads, cities, villages, citing the names and numbers of regiments and companies with which he had fought, giving the exact day and the exact hour of the day of certain occurrences, and send it all to the War Department in Washington.

And when nothing comes of it, he can only hiss, "It's them goddamn rebels." Around the neighborhood he goes, having to hear his rejections read so many times that at last he believes and commits them to his indefatigable memory.

Grandpa and Granny are the comic-tragic extensions of Richard's own mother and father. The men appear slight and quiet, ruined and enduring. The women are filled with a savage Christianity expressing itself in countless slaps and quarrels. But the portrait of the mother is a good deal more than that, the most complicated and the richest in the book. When Du Bois objected that "toward his mother he never expresses love or affection" he acknowledged that Wright continually presents her as the one who beats him. And Ralph K. White in a "Value Analysis" of *Black Boy* for the *Journal of Abnormal and Social Psychology* (October 1947) could contend that Wright "disapproves" of his mother "87 per cent." Whatever that means, and however one does such a thing, Wright's feelings about his mother are rather more complicated.

The book begins with the boy almost dying under the whip of his mother. While she repeatedly beats him into senselessness, Richard could still say, "I had always felt a certain warmth with my mother" for it was she who first "taught me to read, told me stories." And when Richard defies Granny and Aunt Addie, his mother, tottering in and out of sanity, smiled and "rose and hobbled to me on her paralytic legs and kissed me." Richard saw how stroke after stroke, days of hurt in which she wanted only to die, had paralyzed her. His mother's agony touched everything, "gathering to itself all the poverty, the ignorance, the help-lessness; the painful, baffling, hunger-ridden days and hours; the restless moving, the futile seeking, the uncertainty, the fear, the dread; the meaningless pain and the endless suffer-ing." She becomes the central representative figure for the

Negro community in *Black Boy*, embodying all its pain and making its quick, crippled gestures toward release. Richard so identifies with her and with her wounds that

a somberness of spirit that I was never to lose settled over me during the slow years of my mother's unrelieved suffering, a somberness that was to make me stand apart and look upon excessive joy with suspicion, that was to make me self-conscious. . . .

And there is great pathos (which Du Bois could not see, or did not want to admit, and which Ellison found "literary") in the way Richard's mother becomes, like the community, half-crazed with her deprivation.

All these figures and scenes are Wright's effort to take oppression with a seriousness that can expose the full damage. Wright knew that all the evil could not be laid to a man. He refused to create a "white villain." Simon Legree in *Uncle Tom's Cabin* is essentially a fantasy of assimilationism because Mrs. Stowe tries to place in one degraded figure an evil that is pervasive throughout the society. Simon Legree tempts us to think about racism as if it were a personal failure like drunkenness or wife beating. In *Black Boy* we see no villains; we do not even see a series of villains. We see men utterly helpless; varieties of foulness, stunted minds. The villain in *Black Boy* is the depraved consciousness of the white community which has dwarfed itself into a snarling thing.

Fifteen years later, at the Reverend Clayton Williams's American Church in Paris, Wright delivered an address that summarized the portraits of the Southern whites he had presented in *Black Boy*: "Slavery and half-slavery destroyed them as men. You can't burn and castrate the sons of your own fathers and rape the brown daughters who are really your sisters without becoming mad. . . ."

When young Richard works at a white table he marvels at the cruelty of white people toward each other, their compulsive obscenity, their reflexive meanness. Negroes think of the people on the other sides of the tracks as "the white death." And everywhere we look—to Reynolds and Pease in the optical factory, to the white watchman at the hotel, to the storekeepers who cut up the Negro woman, to the men in Memphis who try to get niggers to stab each other for their sport—Wright shows the white world being crushed under "a burden of anxiety and compulsive cruelty." A half-decent white man cannot believe that his workers have beaten Richard and keeps asking "which one" it was. But *Black Boy* shows us it is no "one." Wright discovers that "they did not seem to be individual men, but part of a huge, implacable, elemental design toward which hate was futile." Years later, in his famous speech, "The Ballot or the Bullet," Malcolm X was to say explicitly what Wright's portrait presents implicitly, that black Americans dealing with the white man are "dealing with a man whose bias and prejudice are making him lose his mind, his intelligence, every day." And in this regard *Black Boy* is a book that should upset its white readers far more radically than it often seems to. To be on the side of Richard is to be on the side of life. Of course. It is only when we contend with the death all around him do we see what is centrally important: utter, total sickness. And, seeing that, one can begin to see the dimensions of Wright's indictment.

Reviewers, black and white, objected to the terms of *Black Boy,* for once again Richard Wright was awakening racism as a "beast in the skull." And now he was saying that when the beast took life he took it on all sides, black and white indiscriminately; in the Southern world from which Wright had come, the clawmarks were on everyone. The culture was bleeding to death.

I I I

Commenting on *Black Boy* in *Partisan Review* (Summer 1945) Elizabeth Hardwick said that

in some ways it is a catalogue of all the neurotic compulsions the human being can endure. We have, among other things, pyromania, childhood drunkenness, anal eroticism, somnambulism, and several incidents that threaten to end in family killings.

In this world corroded by hurt, young Richard constantly endures what seem like the vicious and fantastic plots of a deformed mind. "I was a drunkard in my sixth year," he tells us.

I staggered along the pavements, drunk, repeating obscenities to the horror of the women I passed and to the amusement of the men en route to their homes from work.

He was a chronic sleepwalker and "one night I found myself standing in the back yard. The moon was shining bright as day." Throughout the narrative we see him repeatedly paralyzed: on his first day at school "frightened speechless" so that "other children had to identify me, tell the teacher my name and address," then again much later at another school he cannot write his name and "I realized how utterly I was failing and I grew weak and leaned my hot forehead against the cold blackboard" and again at the orphanage office unable to blot envelopes, and even in his early jobs, at the drugstore, unable to respond to orders, he freezes. "My sustained expectation of violence had exhausted me." When Wright would later describe the typical neurosis of the American Negro he would call it "The state of exaggeration"; in his own childhood it is a state of utter immobility.

All life was "like living in a dream, the reality of which might change at any moment." Richard carries around with him a horrid sense of guilt and terror: he burns the house down, kills the stray kitten, gets robbed of the grocery money; he "had the choice of being beaten at home or away from home." His brother says to him, "You did bad," and that is what everybody keeps telling him as he grows up. When he sets fire to the house, he can only see the flames for a moment before he sees "the image of my grandmother lying helplessly upon her bed and there were yellow flames in her black hair." And his mother says, "You didn't stand by that kitten, so why should I stand by you?" So often the words that spill helplessly from his mouth become "something he ought to be killed for." When he peeks into the whore house "evidently I had done something terrible." He concludes that "my life had somehow been full of a nameless wrong, an unatonable guilt."

That the boy could become a writer (or that he could survive with some sanity intact) was almost impossible. On the flyleaf of the first edition of the book we are told, "Remember, reader, that this is the story of an American! American, too, was the hope." That is, here was a story of terrific damage but here was also a story of a humble boy who made it: from log cabin to Honest Abe and from pickaninny to Negro Author. *Black Boy* was redeemed by its myth of eventual triumph. Perhaps it is a myth, but it shows not that any black boy can be a writer (as any poor white boy can be President Honest Abe). We see that a black boy, even in the South, can still be alive at nineteen. The myth of Honest Abe was that a system gave a man the opportunities to go from the bottom to the top of our society; Lincoln's ultimate majesty proved our system worked. The myth of *Black Boy* said that a system had not worked. Wright's wholeness showed the system missed him.

In *Soul on Ice* Eldridge Cleaver is proud to point out that there is no trace of "self-effacing love for his oppressors" in *Native Son*. And, one should add, there is no trace of it in *Black Boy;* though the autobiography does not center, as does the novel, on an act of violence against The Man, the life story itself in an aggressive act, a response not in the patience of "self-effacing" love but in the controlled urgency of masculine pride. To be sure, young Richard does not emerge as a big "bad" man, and he hardly seems to be a candidate for any representative role of "black manhood." Yet that fact raises the crucial question of what Wright is trying to accomplish in *Black Boy*. The answer, I think, involves the quiet, careful terms of self-definition, an insistence on the demands of a genuinely creative ego facing odds of intolerable force. And in this sense the Black Boy may be even harder to face than the Native Son. He is surely less liable to slogans. For all its sustained violence and horrors, there is a certain deep quiet to *Black Boy*. The pride that finally rises up out of its pages does not involve flamboyant acts of destruction. It is a spare, survivor's integrity, poised on the edge of despair. The book comes after Wright had shed the "Bigger" in him, and while there is no relaxing of rage against the system there is an insistence on a sustaining settlement. Which is not to be confused with peace.

Richard's survival was his danger; what most often got him into trouble finally got him out: words. What he says to Granny in the bath, what he writes on all the windows, what he shouts into Uncle Tom's ear, all these are the words he is beaten for. When he first turned to printed words he wanted magic symbols of his own distorted world, a reflection of the violence all around him. "I vowed that as soon as I was old enough I would buy all the novels there were and read them to feed that thirst for violence that was in me, for intrigue, for plotting, for secrecy, for bloody murders." He sought ghastly tales of Bluebeard "hanging his wives by their hair in dark closets" and mad scientists who would lure his victims to a room so that a great machine could suck all the air out and the "victims would die, turning red, blue, then black." Richard said, "This was what I wanted, tales like this." Granny is quite right in her assessment of it as "that Devil stuff." When Richard turns his own hand to composition he begins with "The Voodoo of Hell's Half-Acre." Art imitates life.

But to say that Richard Wright turned to books that would imitate his world is merely to describe a deprived child's hunger for gory fantasy. The magic of words was not a mere reflection of the violence of his world in Bluebeards and mad scientists; words became triumph over that world. Words are the boy's assertion, his way of making the world recognize his existence. Knowing can come to him only out of suffering, and it is all he has to defend himself against that suffering. Words are blood kin to the deprivation they master. Perception stays pain.

Words held for the boy the same thrill that numbers did when he first learned to count, dancing on his bed in his nightclothes, over and over again attaining one hundred. It is the joy of having the pieces come together (as they never came together in his life). Bertrand Russell has remarked that as a child his discovery of Euclid filled him with the pleasure which we usually confine to romantic love. For Richard Wright the discovery of words sent him into ecstasies of control and desire.

Although fear and hunger are the central feelings, there is a third that appears throughout the narrative, and it is vitally important to the characterization (and ultimate victory) of young Richard. That feeling is the shock of surprise. Each time brutality descends on him Richard is, simply, astonished. He cannot learn, cannot toughen himself, cannot get used to it. When Claude Brown and Malcolm X wrote their life stories they presented pictures of depraved worlds, but they also presented themselves as boys "well adjusted" to their worlds. They knew the name of the game. Young Richard never develops the reflexes for easy survival, never seems ready for what comes. His intelligence is large but profoundly unaware, unready. After years of it he still awakens each morning as if this were a first visit. And so he is continually "asking myself what on earth was the matter with me, why it was I never seemed to do things as people expected them to be done." A lady asks him "seriously," "Do you steal?" He laughs aloud because he assumed the lady thought of him as a person: "Lady, if I was a thief, I'd never tell anybody." He is plagued all through his job-hunting days: employers do not want him, do not like the look in his eyes. "Why don't you laugh and talk like the other niggers?" Constantly in trouble for it, "I had to keep remembering what others took for granted; I had to think out what others felt." It was only with the greatest slowness that "I learned to play the dual role which every Negro must play if he wants to eat and live." He refused to give up his mind to the insanity of the compromisers around him.

Words hold it together. Books are dignity, manhood. At the end of the story, when he asks why he had the determination to get out of the Southern darkness, where he had caught "a sense of freedom" in a world where no one had ever asked him to believe in himself, he concludes, "it had been only through books." But he knows that his belief in them "had risen more out of a sense of desperation than from any abiding conviction of their ultimate value." Books satisfied the sense of hunger that he had, the desire for wholeness.

Young Richard continually pesters his mother for names, how did we get them, what do they mean. He wants "just to know" and his mother responds, "but for *what?*" He cannot say. "I could think of no rational or practical reason why my father should try to find out who his father's father was." When he grew to manhood he could think of the reasons. In *Black Boy* he set out on the voyage into knowledge; summoning his best intelligence, he hoped to find meaning and perhaps even some redemption in the chamber of horrors where secrets lie among wounds.

The last word of the first chapter is "knowing." It saved Wright from being like his father, a man who was ruined by not knowing. As "knowing" concludes all the horrors that Wright presents in his opening chapter, so the book itself is an act of "knowing," impelled by the author's "conviction that the meaning of living came only when one was struggling to wring a meaning out of meaningless suffering." *Black Boy* is finally about the realms of the mind, about how the mind is hopelessly conditioned and how it also has a frantic strength to resist conditioning. Wright's ability to come out of it all, and to write about it, is as clear as the world which spent all its energy to see that he never would do it.

CHAPTER 6

The Big Boy Leaves Home

When *Black Boy* was published Richard
Wright was thirty-six, an age when writers
often come into their own, drawing themselves up, ready to demonstrate a full possession of mature power. In *Phylon* the
headline "What Next for Richard Wright?"
was a question that could be asked with
genuine interest and reasonable hope.
What was next was chosen exile and a long
series of often interesting but generally inferior work. In the years up to his death in
1960 we continually find Wright on his
travels, looking for new things in the corners of the world. But he becomes a man
without a country and a writer without
imaginative means. When he returned to
home base, the lovely little apartment at
14 Rue Monsieur le Prince, he could greet

and dine with the famous: Eleanor Roosevelt, Jean Paul Sartre and Simone de Beauvoir, Gunnar Myrdal, Franklin Frazier. But in the glamour of fame and as an honored guest of the French government, something wrong, something sad, had happened. When visitors and old friends came away, or when tourists caught a glimpse of him at his favorite table in the Café Monaco, they told of a man who still could laugh and argue into the night but who often seemed dazed, lonely, absent. In the late fifties he acquired a small farm at Ailly, on the banks of the Eure—not a river, Wright said, just "a dribble"—and worked on *The Long Dream*. Ollie Harrington, reporting for *Ebony* (February 1961), said that Wright had finally realized here "that above all he was a man of the country." Those little lists of purple prose in *Black Boy* may have been unexceptional as writing, but they came from his heart. And so he puttered in the garden, planting potatoes and corn, peas and beans. When harvest came, he brought baskets of vegetables to his friends. It was a good life, and after the day's work he could sit down and smile at a page of *Native Son* or *Black Boy* in Turkish, in Japanese, in Hebrew.

He had left the southland of his youth to go north looking for freedom; even after all his literary successes he found that there was too much pain in the North; again, he would look for escape. In "Early Days in Chicago," an essay included in *Cross Section, 1945,* he spoke of "my fevered search for honorable adjustment to the American scene." Working, living, "I had embraced the daily horror." But for how long, he wondered, did the nightmare have to go on? And so he decided to investigate the question proposed by R. L. Duffus in his review of *Black Boy* for the New York *Times* (March 4, 1945): "What would Richard Wright have been in a more genial social climate? In France, perhaps?" Wright had taken his first trip outside the United States in

1940, to Mexico, returning by train, stopping in Mississippi to see his father, and then riding on to Chapel Hill to work with Paul Green on the stage version of *Native Son*. In 1945, after his break with the Communist Party, he took a holiday in Quebec. There was a brief, wonderful trip to Paris in 1946, a return to New York in November, and in the following July the Wrights returned to Paris for good. James Baldwin wrote, "he had endured already . . . a long exile in his own country. He must have wondered what the real thing would be like." Wright set out to see, full of expectation. But when Baldwin said good-bye, he thought he could see that it was not going to work out; the parting was "melancholy in the way a theater is melancholy when the run of the play is ended and the cast and crew are about to be dispersed." The show had closed.

In *Black Boy* he had written that "a sense of the two races had been born in me with a sharp concreteness that would never die until I died." But perhaps it did not always have to be quite that sharp. Roi Ottley, in *No Green Pastures* quotes Wright as declaring that "there is more freedom in one square block of Paris than in all of the United States." Being a Negro in America had been a full-time job, and he now had decided to retire. In an interview with William Gardner Smith for *Ebony*, Wright said, "Every Negro in America carries all through his life the burden of race consciousness like a corpse on his back. I shed that corpse when I stepped off the train in Paris. Half a lifetime is long enough to carry it. I don't intend to pick it up again."

Yet, briefly, he did. On a return to America in 1947 he talked with a reporter from *PM* who ran a story (February 15) headlined "Why Richard Wright Came Back from France." Wright proclaimed, "I *live* here. . . . The French are in France and the Americans are in America. My work is here. My main job is in this country. I'd like to visit there often, but I belong here. No, I was fashioned in this peculiar kind of hell." But during those months back on native ground he began to ask himself if it had to continue to be that hellish. Living alone in America as a black man was hard enough; living with a white wife and family was unbearable. A century before, Herman Melville had written in *Redburn*:

In Liverpool indeed the negro steps with a prouder pace, and lifts his head like a man; for here, no such exaggerated feeling exists in respect to him, as in America. Three or four times, I encountered our black steward, dressed very handsomely, and walking arm in arm with a good-looking English woman. In New York, such a couple would have been mobbed in three minutes; and the steward would have been lucky to escape with whole limbs.

In the intervening century the sickness had not died. Often the penalty was maddeningly mean—to go into a snack shop with a white woman and be served salted coffee. And there was always the possibility of deeper trouble, the kind Melville described, for gangs were pulling interracial couples out of taxicabs stopped for a light, pulling a black man away from a white woman on the sidewalks, beating them in the street. In the Greenwich Village apartment house the Wrights purchased they were getting it from both sides—from the neighbors who threw constant insults and from a tenant, a former comrade, who organized a rent strike. Both as a black man and as an ex-Communist Wright found living in America next to impossible. Especially troubling was the sight of his daughter, Julia, who was beginning to show some sense of the pain. Wright said, "I feel certain that she knows much more than she knows she knows. . . ." Surely the abrasive and constant hurt, for himself and for his family, had to be stopped. And so, with the invitation from the French government to visit as an honored guest, what had originally been planned as an experiment and an eye opener became a new life. When Willie Morris met Wright years later in Paris he asked, "Will you ever come back to America?" Wright said no.

The native son, the black boy from Mississippi, spent the rest of his life as an adopted citizen of France. And the work in exile, book after book, was voluminous. But as he sent these new books back across the seas, critics began to feel that the serenity he had chosen for himself had severely damaged his writing. While the man was surviving in peace, the tight hard center of the talent was getting unwound. If there are no second acts in the dramas of American writers' lives, the work of Richard Wright in France seemed to prove the rule in his case. Reviewing *The Long Dream* for the New York *Times* (October 26, 1958), Saunders Redding would speak of Wright as if he were already dead, calling (rather cruelly) in the last line: "Come back, Dick Wright, to life again!" And younger black writers did not know exactly what to think. The master, the idol, had gone off and left them to fight the battle alone. Was he quitting in the middle of the battle or was he taking the rest that a great general deserved? Conrad Kent Rivers's poem "To Richard Wright," in the *Antioch Review* (Winter 1960–1961), embodies the contradictory feelings so many were expressing. Rivers accuses: "You hurriedly wrote a book, caught a boat that sails, and sleep soundly." He gets nasty: "I hope that you bask on the Riviera, / and teach your children the non-sensitivity of Caviar." He says Wright is out of touch with the changes: "We are no longer victims of your hate and our color." But in the last lines the young poet suddenly wonders if the old man was right after all, that there is nothing to be done: "You should come back and reappraise . . . but in case you don't / please find room for me over there." When the poem reached print, Wright was dead.

II

Of the eight books produced in France, four were non-fiction: *Black Power* (1954), *The Color Curtain: A Report on the Bandung Conference* (1956), *Pagan Spain* (1957), and *White Man, Listen!* (1957). The last is a collection of lectures delivered between 1950 and 1956; the other three are travel books, and they all begin with variations on the question, Well, why *not* go? *Pagan Spain* opens with Gertrude Stein on her deathbed, muttering, "Dick, you ought to go to Spain." *The Color Curtain* begins at Christmastime with Wright reading about the Bandung Conference in the newspaper, hearing "the call of race," and his wife saying, "If you feel that way, you have to go." And *Black Power* opens on Easter Sunday, with the wife of George Padmore, the West Indian author, asking him, "Why don't you go to Africa?" Three books begin with three women saying, Go, see for yourself.

Black Boy had been a voyage into the South of his youth, a voyage back into the old land and the hearts of the people who lived on it, a voyage in which Wright would speak with utter authority. In the three voyages into unknown territory he would speak as a man unsure of just where he was going, a rootless man hunting for a home in Europe, Africa, Asia. He portrays himself as a very private man, always going it alone. He does not take the family, and has no good close friends to keep him company. He is a little lost. In *Black Power* an African whore accosts him on the street; when he turns her down she says, "Haven't you got a friend who'd be nice to me?" His reply, "I have no friends in Africa," is painful. Later he thinks wistfully of just how alone he really has become, and a phrase from Nietzsche floats up into his mind—"the pathos of distance."

In *La Force des Choses* Simone de Beauvoir wrote of Richard Wright—the time seems to be about 1956—that *"il semblait se désintéresser de la littérature."* And the prose of these four books shows a man who does not have literature much on his mind. He turns again and again to stale figures: "Man's world today lies in the pythonlike coils of vast irrational forces which he cannot control," and leaps into capitalization:

What rivets my attention in this clash of East and West is that an irrational Western world helped, unconsciously and unintentionally to be sure, to smash the irrational ties of religion and custom and tradition in Asia and Africa. THIS, IN MY OPINION, IS THE CENTRAL HISTORIC FACT!

When he quotes Myrdal as head of the Economic Commission of the United Nations he says, "Sounds like the blueprint for a Soviet, huh?" And then he can say, "Oughtn't they to think of taking decades to build a nation, yea, centuries even?" Two words in those sentences—"huh" and "yea"—are the index of the problem in his prose. On the one hand it is shirt-sleeves writing, pull up the chair and let's talk the politiki; on the other hand, he slips into passionate exhortation and old-fashioned fancy talk. Wright was not an elegant essayist, like Baldwin, able to fashion an intense, suave, intellectual style that conveys a formidable personal voice. In his journalism he relies on slang, bombast, and general rhetorical puff to get him over unfamiliar ground. "We have been tramping through an unknown country," he will say; and the prose shows it only too clearly.

He had always been careless with detail, and that carelessness is especially bothersome when he claims to be a reporter putting hard facts before us. In *Pagan Spain,* on page four, he cannot understand whether the Civil Guard

officer beside him in the car wants him to stop or step on it;
there is a big mix-up. Yet a few pages later, on that same
day, when he cannot distinguish between stop and go, a girl
presents him with her "famous green book" of the fascist
catechisms and Wright exclaims, "My Spanish was vague,
but I gaped at the sentiments I saw there in cold type." A
few hours before, his Spanish was not "vague"; it was non-
existent. Such little details are unimportant in themselves
but part of a general lack of authority; too often we feel we
are in the hands of an amateur. On each voyage we are told
about all the interesting books he has been reading; he
"bones up" like a tourist. In *The Color Curtain* there is a
phony sense of urgency as he keeps telling us, "The express
pounded on into the night," and he looks over returned
questionnaires. His conclusions are often schoolbookish:
"There resided deep in her a latent, unconscious ambivalence towards that religion that found expression in her
questioning attitude toward Malaya and her father. She was
hostile toward authority. . . ." And when he gets to Indo-
nesia he can do little more than offer accounts of the ses-
sions, bon mots from the delegates, quotations from the
newspapers, theories by social scientists at MIT refuting
Dutch social scientists. The trouble persists in *Pagan Spain,*
where the book too often disintegrates into barrages of
questionnaire materials or lists; the dialogue does not sound
like dialogue. He asks a horticulturist about produce, and
learns

"Cereals, fruits, and garden produce; add oranges, grapes and
olives and you've almost covered the agricultural side. Otherwise, we have a little coal, iron, and steel. But, you see, our
whole economic structure is lopsided. Our agriculture is still
mainly primitive. We have but little power and less transport,"
he recited. "No matter what they tell you in Madrid, our production is below that of 1935."

"Your facts tally with what I heard from United Nations people in Geneva," I told him. "What has been the effect of Franco's freezing of wages?"

What has gone wrong here is Wright's inability to present himself as in any way qualified by training or familiarity with his subjects so that we should be eager to listen to him. In *Pagan Spain* there are often interesting touches—the mad woman, Lola, and her dog, Ronnie, the funny and sad little train ride in chapter twenty-seven—but they remain "touches" only. Here and there Wright gets the feel of Spain's military sorrow, its hunger, all retreating into the diseases and religion of the past. But these insights and intuitions are rare; most of the time we get travelogue: "The cathedral was a choir of singing stone; rich, ornate, filled with paintings by Goya and Bayeu, etc., it abounded in marble, bronze, alabaster, silks, satins, silver, and gold."

Black Power, the first of the books, is perhaps the only one that could have been a truly successful effort, going beyond slapdash journalism to a sustained and legitimately interesting piece of work. It is far too lengthy a book, in need of editing, but it is also the single book that is held together by more than observation and anecdote. The author has something important to say and some credentials that make us want to join him on the voyage. Or, more accurately, Wright's lack of credentials become his credentials, for he is trying to find some answer to the question in Countee Cullen's poem affixed as one of his epigraphs:

> One three centuries removed
> From the scenes his fathers loved,
> Spicy grove, cinnamon tree,
> What is Africa to me?

In *The Wretched of the Earth* Fanon wrote that "the Negroes of Chicago only resemble the Nigerians or the

Tanganykans in so far as they were all defined in relation to the whites." While that definition was overpoweringly enforced, the facts were that:

The test cases of civil liberty whereby both blacks and whites in America try to drive back racial discrimination have very little in common in their principles and objectives with the heroic fight of the Angolan people against the detestable Portuguese colonialism. The problems which kept Richard Wright and Langston Hughes on the alert were fundamentally different from those which might confront Leopold Senghor or Jomo Kenyatta.

And Richard Wright had continually resisted even the racial definition. In *Pagan Spain* he said, "I have no race except that which is forced upon me. I have no country except that to which I'm obliged to belong. I have no traditions." He objected to "reverse racism" in *The Color Curtain*. His theme is continually: "Color is not my country . . . I am opposed to all racial definitions." And in *Black Power* he confesses "my kind of thinking was impotent when it came to explaining life in 'racial terms.'" Yet perhaps, perhaps, there *was* something in color, something that could make him understand his lost homeland and feel a kinship with Africans. But he discovered in the Gold Coast how meager a bond the color was. It was a source of great dismay, running through the book as a sense of loneliness, separation:

I was black and they were black, but my blackness did not help me.

I'm of African descent and I'm in the midst of Africans, yet I cannot tell what they are thinking and feeling.

One did not leave the past behind; one took it with one; one made the past the present. I could not get beyond that, for it was alien to me; it was intriguing, but beyond the bounds of my feelings. I could understand it, but I couldn't experience it.

. . . faced with the absolute otherness and inaccessibility of this new world, I was prey to a vague sense of mild panic. . . .

He keeps trying to find something that will connect him, join him to his African friends. Dr. Danquah asks him:

> "How long have you been in Africa?"
> "About two months," I said.
> "Stay longer and you'll *feel* your race," he told me.
> "What?"
> "You'll *feel* it," he assured me. "It'll all come back to you."
> "What'll come back?"
> "The knowledge of your race."

But it does not. When Malcolm X returned to America after visiting Nigeria he could say with pride that the Muslim Students Society renamed him "Omowale"—"the child has come home" in Yoruba. For Richard Wright, no. Some of the most amusing and touching passages in *Black Power* are those in which Wright shows himself desperately reaching out, imitating, trying to get with it, and failing every time:

> Young and old, men and women, people of high and low stations in life, spit. I observed a young girl of about twelve years of age for about five minutes and she spat six times. And this spitting is not just ordinary spitting; it's done in a special manner. First, taut lips are drawn back over clenched teeth, and from out through the clenched teeth comes a jet of saliva, straight, clean, strong, like a bullet from a gun, never touching the lips. The people do not seem to be ill; I've seen no one chewing tobacco or dipping snuff. Is this spitting at all times and in all places a kind of reflex? Or does the climate here engender a universal catarrhal condition . . . ? I tried, before my mirror in my hotel room with the door locked, to spit like that and I succeeded only in soiling the front of my shirt. . . .

Black Power is the only one of these books which comes to any real terms with the problem behind them all, Wright's sense of exclusion, wandering, rootlessness. *Black*

Power is in many ways a poignant book, and that accounts for both its strength and its weakness. *Black Boy* had been subtitled "A Record of Childhood and Youth"; *Black Power* was "A Record of Reactions in a Land of Pathos." But the "land of pathos" was in Wright's own heart, as he drifted. His ancestral homeland is a foreign country. He looks around, and it is all so extremely odd. The penalty for adultery by a royal person is two hundred pounds, seven sheep, and two cases of gin. For a Mohammedan it is five pounds five shillings, one hundred kola nuts, and one piece of white shirting material. Wright laughs.

Like the other reports from foreign lands, *Black Power* is a book written by a man on the move, full of energy for questioning, gathering facts, seeking out everyone who will talk to him. Up early, he is out with his camera and note-book. But when it is time for the final assessment, when he has to bring it all together, there is a sense of quiet despera-tion and confusion that maybe all the energy was trying to keep him from confronting. The superstitions of the Gold Coast had held her back from so much; yet (the punctuation. is Wright's):

It may be that such beliefs fit the soul of man better than rail-roads, mass production, wars. . . . And the African is not alone in holding that these dreams are true. All men, in some form or other, love these dreams. Maybe men are happier when they are wrapped in warm dreams of being with their fathers when they die . . . ?

III

Wright published three novels after he left America: *Savage Holiday, The Outsider,* and *The Long Dream. Sav-age Holiday* was rejected by Harper's, and Wright's agent, Paul Reynolds, agreed with the editorial decision: it was inferior work that wouldn't sell and could only harm Wright's reputation. In order to protect the long-standing contract with Harper's, the manuscript was not submitted to any other hard-cover house, and was sold to Avon as a paperback original. Wright's reputation was not on the line since the paperback did not go through the normal reviewing and promotional channels.

The novel is a small and improbable story set in New York; the characters are all white (and, indeed, Wright said that he wanted it published under a pseudonym so that no one would know that a black man had written it). In *Savage Holiday* a Puritan and his neighbor on the floor below, an Easy Woman, are jointly responsible for the death of the Easy Woman's little boy. The Puritan, locked out of his apartment without any clothes on (as he was reaching for the Sunday paper) rides frantically down in the elevator to get a pass key, sees people coming to the elevator, rides back up, and tries to get into his apartment by climbing up from the balcony below. The child, playing on the balcony, sees a naked man and faints, falling several stories to the street below. The boy is wildly terrified of naked men because his mother always neglected to close the door during her jaunty amours and the son peered in and thought the naked men were "fighting" his mother on the bed, trying to kill her.* The Puritan gets safely into his apartment without anyone

---

* It's all taken care of in Chester Himes's *Pinktoes:* ". . . their daughter, Marilyn, came into the room and saw Papa bouncing up and down on top of Mama while Mama was gasping and moaning and crying and trying to throw Papa off, the way it looked to her. Naturally she thought they were fighting. So what can you tell a child in a case like this? Art said they were working up a sweat in order to take a bath. So Marilyn said, Oh, goody-goody, I'll run the water. So Art had to get up and take a bath." *Pinktoes* is a very funny book, and the work of Chester Himes—widely known in Europe—deserves much more attention in this country than it has so far received.

seeing him, but in his guilt he keeps calling on the Easy Woman, trying to get her to marry him. They will make, he thinks, a new bright son to atone for the one that they both, in their ways, killed. But the Easy Woman senses something wrong, keeps pushing him to find out what it is, and finally he goes out of his mind, stabs her to death, and turns himself in. It has all been a *Savage Holiday*.

The book is heavily loaded with "psychology." The made-to-order dreams are embarrassingly bad:

He pushed farther on into the forest and then he was suddenly afraid and hid himself behind a large tree and listened to the sound of *whack whack whack* somebody was in the forest chopping down one of his trees and he peered cautiously and saw a tall man swinging a huge ax chopping furiously into a v-shaped hollow. . . .

And when at the end of the story all the details come together like the end of a bad detective yarn: the clue, the missing part, here it is and now my tale is done. All through the narrative Erskine keeps playing with colored pencils that he carries with him. On the final pages Wright takes us back into Erskine's childhood nightmare of Gladys and Mommie and the mutilated doll; as Erskine thinks of how he killed Mommie by proxy with the colored pencils Wright tells us in italics, *"He now understood the four pencils!"* And so, alas, do we.

When *The Outsider* appeared, a critic writing for the *Crisis* said the book "stands like a titan among the major works of the twentieth century." Orville Prescott, still sitting there at the New York *Times*, said in his review (March 18, 1953) that here Wright was going down a whole new road; perhaps he had located "one of the symptoms of the intellectual and moral crisis of our times." Over at the *Herald Tribune* Wright was featured on the front page of the Book

Review, a large portrait of him brooding in front of a high overflowing bookshelf; Granville Hicks's decision was that Wright's hero, Cross Damon, spoke for modern man. His "principal problems have nothing to do with his race. They are pre-eminently the problems of the human being as such" and the novel "challenges the modern mind." Wright had broken out of the narrow range of Negro writing to present a symbolic extravaganza of metaphysical dilemmas.

The plot of *The Outsider* is similar to that of *The Chips Are Down,* the work of Wright's new friend, Jean Paul Sartre. They are both stories of the unused life, the incomplete, the blank waiting to be filled. In Wright's version, Cross Damon (Crucified Devil) works in the post office (Kierkegaard's image of the postman as Christian). There is an existentialist burning of the Old Faith (the Church Militant, no less, for the Selective Service office is in the basement). The two political temptations of modern man are presented in a Fascist and a Communist, locked in a death struggle with a poker; the Outside Man kills them both, impartially, and then falls in love with an artistic girl named Eva (primal, creative) but she commits suicide and leaves him alone at the mercy of Ely Houston, the D.A. (Dostoevsky's psychological detective). At the end, as Cross dies, there is a nod to Mr. Yeats ("the myth men are going . . . the real men, the last men are coming . . .") and a nod to Mr. Conrad:

His eyes stared bleakly. His effort was supreme; his lips parted; his tongue moved; he cursed that damned ball of seething fire that raged in his chest and managed to get his reluctant breath past it to make words;

"It . . . was . . . horrible. . . ."

Wright seems to have felt that something was wrong; on March 17, 1953, he wrote to Jack Fischer at Harper's: "I hope you're keeping your fingers crossed as I am for luck for Cross; he needs it!"

Our hero's recent past included "attending day classes at the University of Chicago, majoring in Philosophy and working the night shift in the Post Office." And the ideas in the novel are those of a student. We find introductory psychology and popularized existentialist jargon everywhere throwing the characters into action, but never clarifying them or their relationships to each other. Wright's talent had always been to explore racial nightmares in scenes of racial violence, to see the meaning in bone-crushing tortures. In *The Outsider* he gives us four murders and a suicide, scenes of destruction that equal in frenzy anything in his earlier work; the novel constantly tops itself in grisly shocks. But where there had been an idea impelling all the violence in his previous fiction, now the violence was staged so that certain observations could be made about modern man and metaphysical realities. And if one had not encountered Wright's earlier work, this novel would seem to be the product of a mind incapable of control, paranoid and suicidal.

In *The Color Curtain* Wright said of one of the men who returned his questionnaire: "I have the impression that ideas are more real to him than reality." In *The Outsider* the "ideas" are supposed to be the reality, yet Wright cannot bring them to life in the characters who represent them and orate them. Throughout the narrative we find a severely unfinished prose, "unwritten" scenes, a writer's notes to himself. He often seems to be saying, let us pause now for another idea of mine:

He realized that this blue-jazz was a rebel art blooming seditiously under the condemnations of a Protestant ethic just as his own consciousness had sprung conditioned to defiance from his relationship to his mother. . . .

When we need some information about the little girl, Eva, Wright pastes up a diary that in no way convinces us it is a

diary, filled with such entries as: "After father died when I
was six, I lived in that orphan's home." And when Cross
says, standing over the bodies of the Fascist and the Communist, "I killed two little gods," we can only say, Yes, of
course you did, because you are THE OUTSIDER.

Wright said, "My hero could have been of any race." And
he obsessively insists upon it. When Sarah asks Cross when
he joined the colored race; he replies, "I never joined."
When Cross has the opportunity to live again, "there was no
racial tone to his reactions; he was just a man, *any* man who
had had an opportunity to flee and had seized upon it."
Later on we learn of his decision that "his consciousness of
the color of his skin had played no role in it." In a café a
tall man says, "For four hundred years these white folks
done made everybody on earth feel like they ain't human,
like they're *outsiders*." But Wright is not exploring, here,
that outsideness. Cross seeks men who were "outsiders not
because they had been born black and poor, but because
they had thought their way through the main veils of illusion." And for Cross Damon, "being a Negro was the least
important thing in his life."

Cross Damon "was fleeing to escape his identity, his old
hateful consciousness," and so was Richard Wright. He was
trying to break new ground. He did not want to do another
book on "the Problem"; it was time for a novel that would
be judged simply as "novel." Color could be a curse, but it
also could be a crutch; and now he would walk on his own
feet, without the responsibility of being, that phrase so often
applied to him, "an eloquent spokesman for his race."

Yet the best things in the book come when Wright does
turn to race. The scenes with his post office cronies do not
send us to Kierkegaard's symbol of the postman as Christian.
Wright had worked in a post office in Chicago and knew
what it was like, could create the Negro men working there

as he had in *Lawd Today*. When in the café the speculation
is sent out that the men from Mars are colored and the
whole universe, except for earth, is run by colored men,

> one black boy danced ecstatically, then, holding his hand over
> his mouth, as though he felt it unseemly to vent his savage mirth
> indoors, ran out of the café, leaving the door open. Upon the
> snowy sidewalk he screamed and howled and flapped his arms
> in the icy wind.

The prose works, conveying the rage and comedy and
physical energy of the fantasy. Similarly, when Cross goes to
get a birth certificate, the characters begin to inhabit a
recognizable world. Cross plays Dumb Nigger. When the
clerk joshes him, "Are you sure you were born?" he responds, "Well, they *say* I was born. If I wasn't born, I can't
keep my job." The clerks ask his name, and he says, "But
you know. They say you got all the names here." Cross does
not have to be anybody because as a darky he knows all
white men "would leap to supply him with a background
and an identity." The whole scene is done with a quick and
bitter comic sense.

In "universalizing" his Negro, Wright had made him less
large. To make Cross black and then keep insisting he was
not really a Negro was only to deny him any cultural
reality or individual coherence. The name "Bigger Thomas"
and the title *Native Son* present a difficult and savage
question; the name "Cross Damon" and the title *The Outsider* nod at significance. The courtroom speech in *Native
Son* deflected our interest; here, the book itself is a long
series of contrived speeches, leading to a twenty-page harangue by Cross: modern man "somehow failed to pronounce the magic talisman correctly when catastrophe descended upon him." No one knows what Eva and Sarah
and Blimin are doing while the pages of oratory roll by.
Surely not listening. "Aye," Cross says, and "now back to my

theme . . . à la Lord Acton." *The Outsider* is in many ways an unconscious parody of Wright's old power. Here we find the same shocks, the same reflexes, the same spurting violence, but all turned loose without any legitimate direction. The novel frequently shows fierce energy, and when the metaphysics are turned off Wright still could write brilliant little stretches and create minor characters of considerable interest. He had not lost his ability for characterization or narrative drive; he no longer knew what his characters meant and where he was driving.

Whenever he had presented sexuality in his previous work it was presented symbolically as an act of violence. In *The Outsider* he gives us several sexual scenes, done as pulp-magazine titillation:

he moved his naked elbow across her left breast, caressing it, gently indenting the soft surrendering flesh under the sheer cloth of her dress as much as he dared, and, this time, he knew that she knew, for he felt the tip of her loose breast gradually hardening, growing delicately into a pointed, taut nipple.

There is too much peek-a-boo: "The nylon gown was pulled taut across the curves of her firm, yellow thighs, and through the sheer white translucence of the tissue he could see the dark smudge of her pubic hair."

In his review for the *New Republic* (May 4, 1953), John Henry Raleigh described the hero of *The Outsider* as "Bigger Thomas intellectualized and gone French Existentialist." Yet if Bigger Thomas were "intellectualized" or existentialist, surely his color would not cease to exist for him (as Wright insists it has ceased to exist for Cross); moving through America he would be even more aware, more anguished, at the curse of color. In his diary Wright noted: "I have to remind myself that I'm a Negro when I live in Paris. There are whole days when I forget it." Forgetting, or refusing to acknowledge, the psychic economics of color in America, he made an Outsider who did not make sense. Wright was trying to go "beyond color." But, as William Carlos Williams has said, "We do not have to abandon our familiar and known to achieve distinction; rather in that place, if only we make ourselves sufficiently aware of it, do we join with others in other places." Color was Richard Wright's "familiar and known"; through it, through his sufficient awareness he had achieved distinction. Color was his way of seeing the world, the energy that enforced his finest perception. When he tried to be colorblind he went, for a dreadful space, blind.

Robert A. Bone has said that the last novel in exile, *The Long Dream*, is "a still more disastrous performance" than *The Outsider*. It is a strange verdict; while *The Long Dream* is a retreat to old ground, it is ground Wright knows well and can cover with considerable authority. The central event of the narrative is probably based on the disaster of the Rhythm Nite Club in Natchez, Wright's old hometown, in April of 1940 (and where Wright was to pass through, a little later that year, on his way back from Mexico). The Rhythm Nite Club was covered with dry Spanish moss, all its windows boarded to keep out nonpaying celebrants. The single entry was the single exit. On April 24, the club burned to the ground, killing two hundred and fifteen. A correspondent for an Afro-American newspaper reported the sight of ninety-eight bodies laid out at a Natchez undertaking parlor. In *The Long Dream* the father of the central character is the owner of a large undertaking establishment, and part owner of the Dance Hall where a fire takes dozens of lives. He is in silent partnership with the white police chief, Cantley; after the disaster we watch the two men work together, to get out from under, the infighting, the demands, the lines drawn, how to cross them, how to cover your rear. The white cop and the black undertaker hold the black and white communities together in a grotesque, dirty deal.

In 1930 Richard Wright had gone all over the South Side of Chicago, to hundreds of little slum dwellings; he was working as an agent for a Negro burial society. He would use his memories of that job in his portrait of the boy, Fishbelly—whose name is the title of the French edition of *The Long Dream*—out collecting for his dad. Wright discovered that many "comely black housewives" were willing to have affairs with him in exchange for the payment of their policy premiums. One of the girls he tells about always wanted him to take her to a circus. Racial degradation, burial societies, sordid sex are all brought together in *The Long Dream*, often as a kind of circus, a carnival side show which is always threatening to burn to the ground. Wright frequently punctuates the narrative with scenes of strange, twisted comedy, achieving in the grotesque humor the tone that characterizes the best of his last work in the posthumous collection, *Eight Men*.

Early in the book Fishbelly and his pals go to a carnival where one banner proclaims: "HIT THE NIGGER HEAD, Three Baseballs for 50¢." Various white men step up to "knock that nigger's brains out." Fifty yards away, chained up, his head poking through a hole in thick canvas, a black boy flips his head, dodges, and cries high obscene laughter. Fishbelly is so ashamed at the way the boy has degraded himself, that he buys three balls and tries to hit him, as delighted whites cry, "Nigger hitta nigger." The whites buy balls for the black boys, and one of Fish's friends, Tony, finally succeeds in bloodying the black head as the whites respond with "an orgiastic cheer." As the boys walk away in angry desperation—Fishbelly churning with the fear that the "obscene black face was his own face"—one of the women in the girlie show tries to get them all in to her darkened trailer: " 'I'll take you in for five dollars apiece,' she said, unbuttoning her blouse and baring her big white breasts in the half-light." The boys tear home, horrified: "Goddamn, man! That sure was lynch-bait!"

The scene embodies the central techniques and themes of the novel as a whole: the carnival, the racial oppression, the sexuality, the danger. The boys spend an evening in the funeral parlor basement, talking of the problem in keeping a dead body black, how not to let it get "waxy and rosy." Sometimes, Fish says, his father had to paint the corpses so their folks would accept them. A big problem was gas on the stomach: "Sometimes so much gas gits in a dead man's belly that he sits up straight and hollers!" The grisly comedy continues when Fish is arrested and keeps fainting in the police station; the cops enjoy the show: "Goddamn, that nigger's eyes turned into his head like a window shade going up." They bring the lieutenant in, and he asks, "Is it a trick, or does he really faint?" The boy goes through his routine, in terror, blacking out. It is like the carnival, a section of a circus nightmare. And Fishbelly himself is often sick, in swamps of fever, paralyzed by hallucinations (that often seem to be like delirium tremens, the kind of dreams that an author who had been a drunkard in his sixth year might have lived through):

In a corner of his room stood a giant, magically luminous spider whose thin, frizzy legs curved downward into blackness, its baglike body seemingly filled with a dangerous fluid held precariously in a delicate, transparent membrane. Stricken, he watched the spider's roving, glowing eyes and saw the long, fuzzy legs beginning to move and the trembling, sacklike body, weighted with liquid, inching implacably forward, heading for him.

The Long Dream is a long nightmare.

Tyree, the father, advises his son: "Dream, Fish. But be careful what you dream. Dream only what can happen.

. . ." In his early years the boy thinks of his father as a dirty Uncle Tom: "He knew in a confused way that no white man would ever need to threaten Tyree with castration; Tyree was already castrated." But gradually, as he works with his father and senses the pressures he is under, Fishbelly begins to think that his father has achieved all that an illiterate black man could in the South. And when the fire at the whore house puts them in deep trouble, Fishbelly wants to fight shoulder to shoulder with his father—the man who cannot read, the richest man in darktown. The boy begins to love his father in a scene of sexual education—Tyree takes Fish to the whore house—and there occurs an incredibly sad, lovely, and outrageously comic scene. The father, who owns half the place (and who will eventually be killed for it), is proud of his son, as they walk back home. The father muses, "Nature's sure wonderful," and then turns:

"Fish, *goddamn!*" Tyree's words crooned and died away deep in his diaphragm.
"What, Papa?"
"Damn, boy! Ha, ha! You can *go!* You took to it like a duck to water! You better'n I was at your age."

"Fish. Think *hard*. Ain't you done completely forgot 'em?"
"Who, Papa?"
"Them goddamn *white* folks."

Richard Wright, who had never created a father figure of any size in his work, and who had been robbed of a father in his own life, puts Tyree at the center of his last novel, a father who can bring his son into sexual manhood, a man of great power, comedy, and love, a desperately sordid and hopeless man with brutal dignity.

But as Fish goes about his father's business he sees the insane degradation of the people who pay Tyree. These are the dirty end of the carnival grotesques, cackling, tortured little people hiding in shacks. Fish concludes, "Papa, this rent collecting's showing me something . . . our folks is *sick*, Papa." And so are the whites, the "huge, mechanical dolls" that Fish encounters. When a black boy is killed, and his mutilated body is brought to the undertaking establishment, Dr. Bruce says:

Those *whites* suffered more than this boy. Only folks who *suffer* can kill like this.

And the police chief shows the suffering in his dealings with Tyree. The top black deals with The Man and the sickness of their partnership destroys them both. The chief actually is "pleading for mercy" as he yells, "GODDAMN YOU, TYREE!" Cantley is a vicious, totally brutalized man; but he is smart and there is some calcified drop of human sympathy in him. He is a prisoner of the law he enforces. All through the narrative, when we see Cantley, we see a man who realizes he is caught up in a fantastically cruel dumb show. "I swear to God, I don't know what we can do with you niggers . . . we make you scared of us, and then we ask you to tell us the truth."

The novel is a *Bildungsroman,* the story of a black boy's gradual discovery of what the Southern community means and the illness that it endures. If that is its strength, it was essentially the same strength of *Black Boy. The Long Dream* does not really take us into any new territory; it re-establishes Wright's claim to the old. *Black Boy* and *The Long Dream* both contain errant fathers, the nightmares of the black child, the murder of a bellhop, the delayed and then crushing encounter with the white community, and the final flight to another world. Fishbelly's story is that of young Richard who gradually grew to know the South, almost to be destroyed by it; and at the end of the novel Fishbelly goes off to a new life in France just as young Richard went off to a new life in Chicago, and then later to France himself.

The original version of *Black Boy* had been a third longer than the book as it was published; Wright had gone on to describe the Chicago adventures before finally deciding the book should end in the South. And so with *The Long Dream*: Wright tried to carry Fish on into Paris, writing six different extensions of the story on into the world of exile, but each version seemed to fall apart as he was writing it. Once again, the South was the place to stop.

The trouble with the new version was that it was not so cleanly written a book as was *Black Boy,* nor is it so consistently alert in its moral attention; Fishbelly's story is overlong, full of speeches, infected with Wright's late tendency to insert pat Freudian symbols, where too often the characters suddenly blurt into spokesmen for the author's message. Where it is good, *The Long Dream* is very good, conveying the harsh dirty world of the South as a surrealistic nightmare, yet Wright is not altogether sure of himself, and pads the narrative, falls into old errors.

Wright would insist that in retelling his story in a slightly new way, variations on a theme, he was only being accurate about the racial conditions in America. When he had returned on another brief visit (to film *Native Son,* in which—an extremely unfortunate decision—he played Bigger Thomas) he would insist that the world had not changed. There was a sameness to racial violence, a sameness to the mental cruelties which impelled it. His friend and old comrade Langston Hughes would say in the summer of 1961 at a symposium on "The Negro in American Culture" that every year when he would travel over much of the country, in spite of progress here and there, "by and large, it seems to me not really very different from when I was a child." And in an interview for *Ebony* (January 1951): "Wright insists little has happened in the U.S. in the field of race relations since he left." As long as America continued to repeat its racism, Wright would continue to repeat his truth about it.

But he was repeating it with less clarity, less disciplined power. The usual complaint was that he had "cut himself off from his roots." On April 30, 1953, Paul Reynolds wrote to Jack Fischer, Wright's editor at Harper's:

> I have been worried for a long while as to what Wright should do. He told his story in fiction in *Native Son* and non-fiction in *Black Boy*. It seemed to me clear that he couldn't live in Paris and write about the Negro problem in America. *The Outsider* showed evidence of a man out of touch. . . ."

Europe was a kind of no man's land for Richard Wright; he wandered in it. Yet perhaps Reynolds was more accurate in saying that Wright had a single story to tell, not that he was "out of touch." Even if he had stayed in America, what could he have gone on to do after *Native Son* and *Black Boy*? The end of *The Long Dream* was often quoted by reviewers as evidence that Wright's language had gone bad on him in exile. Fishbelly had been trapped, as so often Wright's black boys were, in a bedroom with a white woman. The police had sent her there, and staged a "rape." After agonizing months in jail, Fish gets out and limps onto a plane bound for Paris (where his old buddies, now in the service, live and promise him freedom). Winging over the Atlantic, Fishbelly

> peered out of his window and saw vast, wheeling populations of ruled stars swarming in the convened congresses of the skies anchored amidst nations of space and he prayed wordlessly that a bright, bursting tyrant of living sun would soon lay down its golden laws to loosen the locked legions of his heart and cast the shadow of his dream athwart the stretches of time.

Now the language is surely going up in balloons; but the stars were twinkling there long before Richard Wright went to France, and *Black Boy* had ended with its own rhetorical flourish:

I headed North, full of a hazy notion that life could be lived with dignity, that the personalities of others should not be violated, that men should be able to confront other men without fear or shame, and that if men were lucky in their living on earth they might win some redeeming meaning for their having struggled and suffered here beneath the stars.

The two passages may show how far Wright had fallen, but rhetorical puffery had always been a danger with him, and it was no foreign disease he had contracted. He had caught it on native ground.

Richard Wright did not go away and cut off his roots; he went away because he was tired, weary of facing the curse for thirty-six years. *Uncle Tom's Children, Native Son* and *Black Boy* were written; they were the stories he had to tell. If he had tried to portray the folk culture he would have come up against the fact that he did not adequately know it, as his few efforts at writing "blues" lyrics show only too well. In *Black Power* he confessed that "Never in my life had I been able to dance more than a few elementary steps, and carrying of even the simplest tune had always been beyond me." Black Boy didn't have natural rhythm. He had what he had done.

If he had turned to the essay, again, he would probably have been in trouble. Lionel Trilling's review of *Black Boy* for the *Nation* (April 7, 1945) was perhaps the best review Wright ever received; in a single page Trilling eloquently presented a thorough understanding of what Wright's accomplishment had been, and he gave a suggestion as to what the author might profitably have gone on to try in future work. Trilling said that the story of how a fresh, relatively uneducated man comes to the city—the "Young Man from the Provinces" theme—was always a subject of "the richest moral interest" and that Richard Wright was perhaps capable of telling a sequel to *Black Boy* in which we could see his further adventures, how he grew up to participate in the main cultural streams of national life. The further adventures of Black Boy, what happened to him in the industrial North, the struggle with the Party, the emergence into literary fame, all could be part of an important story.

Had Wright followed this advice he would have been able to save himself from the disasters of *The Outsider,* perhaps, but from the evidence it is unlikely that he would have been able to equal the success of *Black Boy.* His essay "Early Days in Chicago" is, in fact, the first part of what Trilling had suggested, a continuation of the story. The incidents are good in themselves, but Wright's interpretation is often unsure, and when we reach the end we feel that the incidents are too anecdotal, run on, without the pressure of the Southern environment in *Black Boy* to hold them together. What he had to say about the Party he said in "I Tried to Be a Communist"; the Party figure in *Native Son* had been an angel and the Party figures in *The Outsider* were devils. But he had trouble making them men, bringing them to any subtle or carefully observed life. Had he gone on to the "Further Adventures of Black Boy" he would have written a book of secondary interest.

Wright's genius was the ability to create a sharp brutal picture, or series of pictures, that embodies one overpowering image of racial outrage. In his finest stories, in *Native Son,* and in *Black Boy,* he played it close to the line, relentlessly exploring the terror in a single figure, making us participate with that figure in his terror, and giving us a significant meaning in that terror. What made Wright so alert to that emotion, the emotion at the center of all his finest writing, also made him singularly unfit to do other jobs. The story he was equipped to tell was a narrow one, but a very deep one; after he had presented it in his central metaphors there was no new ground he could cover. At Wright's death, from the manuscripts left on his table, Herbert Hill published "Five Episodes" in his anthology *Soon One Morning.* The episodes are about Fishbelly in France, all sharp and clear little images but without any important connecting sense behind them, undemonstrative of large importance. Like the unfinished manuscripts of Hawthorne's last phase, these pieces of a novel show all the old gifts without the old understanding.*

It is hard to see why Wright should have stayed in America of the 1950's or what America of that time had to offer him. The black man's struggle was beginning to be the Civil Rights Movement. Wright had tried political action in the Party, and the new movement was not likely to claim him—not in its nonviolence, not in its profoundly Christian appeal to the conscience of the nation. He had written in 1945, in "Early Days in Chicago,"

I feel that for white America to understand the significance of the problem of the Negro will take a bigger and tougher America than any we have yet known. I feel that America's past is too shallow, her national character too superficially optimistic, her very morality too suffused with color hate for her to accomplish so vast and complex a task. Culturally the Negro represents a paradox: though he is an organic part of the nation, he is excluded by the entire tide and direction of American culture. Frankly, it is felt to be right to exclude him, and it is felt to be wrong to admit him freely. Therefore if, within the confines of its present culture, the nation ever seeks to purge itself of its color hate, it will find itself at war with itself, convulsed by a spasm of moral confusion. If the nation ever finds itself examining its real relations to the Negro, it will find itself doing infinitely more than that; for the anti-Negro at-

* Such a judgment may need to be considerably revised, however, if Ellen Wright decides to release the entire novel manuscript, "Island of Hallucinations."

titude of whites represents but a tiny part—though a symbolically significant one—of the moral attitude of the nation. Our
too-young and too-new America, lusty because it is lonely, aggressive because it is afraid, insists upon seeing the world in
terms of good and bad, the holy and the evil, the high and the
low, the white and the black; our America is frightened by fact,
by history, by processes, by necessity. It hugs the easy way of
damning those whom it cannot understand, of excluding those
who look different; and it salves its conscience with a self-
draped cloak of righteousness. And I really do not think that
America, adolescent and cocksure, a stranger to suffering and
travail, an enemy of passion and sacrifice, is ready to probe into
its most fundamental beliefs.

He saw what continued residence in America could mean;
perhaps in France he could save himself and his family from
additional meaningless pain. The title of one of the books
he would write in exile, *Black Power,* would not furnish
until after his death the slogan for that movement to which
a Richard Wright could return, if indeed he ever could
return. And if he had seen America for what it was, in the
above passage, then by 1945 his story had been told.

I V

The stories brought together in the posthumously published *Eight Men* are gathered from as early as the *Masses*
in 1937 and as late as *Esquire* in 1957. Equally divided
between work done in America and in France, the pieces
range from the briefly quiet little blues tune on "The
Man Who Saw the Flood," a story of a helplessly dazed
Negro family at the mercy of nature and the White Man,
to the wildly comic (and often merely silly) dialogues of
"Man, God Ain't Like That," in which the superstitious
African disciple can take bloody revenge on his white Lord,
"Now it's *black man's* turn!" Wright speaks in his own

voice for the essay on "The Man Who Went to Chicago" and enters into the mind of a white Danish hotel manager who wets his pants at the sight of the monstrous "Big Black Good Man." From story to story, and often in a single story itself, Wright's tone (and control) varies considerably: he can be light, feather-light, merely fooling around with French detectives, then driving along a brutal line of sheer physical torment, or entering the nightmare of urban life or playing variations on his familiar theme of a rural black boy in the South, destroyed by his own ignorance and white prejudice. *Eight Men* is a representative selection, showing the variety of Richard Wright's talent and the course of its development over twenty years of work.

Two of the stories, "The Man Who Lived Underground" and "Man of All Work," achieve the level of his very best. The first originally appeared in *Accent* (Spring 1942) and was then enlarged for *Cross Section, 1944*; it has the narrative drive he had demonstrated in *Native Son*, enriched with the care and control he was to demonstrate in *Black Boy* a year later. "Man of All Work" is a very late story (the germ of which came from an incident Wright had read about in *Jet*), presenting the encounter between white woman and black man; but for one last time he would treat it as comedy. Here, toward the end, he was experimenting with comic drama, as in his translation and adaptation of Louis Sapin's "Daddy Goodness." The hilarity of "Man of All Work" and the grim horror of "The Man Who Lived Underground" call to each other across a decade, indicating Wright's best accomplishments at home and on foreign ground. In the earlier work we look up from a manhole into the pistol barrel of the white world; in the other we look back in laughter at the bathrooms and kitchens of an absurd master race.

"The Man Who Lived Underground" (which is so clearly influenced by Dostoevsky's "Notes from Underground" and which in turn so clearly influenced Ellison's *Invisible Man*) begins with the cry, "I've got to hide." The man is "tired of running and dodging" the white man's law. Faced with the choice of "hide or surrender," the black man in America goes underground. The sewer is Wright's metaphor for the black ghetto, a dank place crawling with rats. Wright chose to end his essay on "The Man Who Went to Chicago":

The hospital kept us four Negroes as though we were close kin to the animals we tended, huddled together down in the under-world corridors of the hospital, separated by a vast psychological distance from the significant processes of the rest of the hos-pital—just as America had kept us locked in the dark under-world of American life for three hundred years. . . .

The Everyblackman with whom we experience the story is Wright's exemplary figure for the timeless suffering of the race. In the sewer he thinks "he had been down here a long time," when he went down he held on for "an eternal moment," and continually he will escape any particular time to stand "for what seemed to him a thousand years."

Somewhere back there, long ago, he had signed a con-fession of guilt. He was bad. He was black because he was bad, bad because he was black. "He had been too tired when they had shouted at him, demanding that he sign his name; he had signed it to end his pain." The white men do not care if he is guilty or not; they only want to use him. "In-nocent, he felt guilty, condemned." And so he descends.

The descent is madness: on the way in he bashes his head against a wall, and when he comes out again he can only laugh with "abandoned glee." Throughout his long stay in the sewer he is constantly seeing things as visions in a grotesque nightmare, "something abysmally obscene" (the adverb is accurate):

hearing a feathery cadence which he could not identify . . .

his fingers toyed in space, like the antennae of an insect . . .

a rich lather bloomed in his cupped fingers, like a scarlet sponge . . .

And when he falls asleep, into his own nightmares, the visions can achieve merely equal grotesqueness. In the sewer of the ghetto, life appears in symbolic pairs: a baby's body blossoming in water and a corpse in an undertaking establishment, spiritual disciplines of the church and spiritual relaxations of the movie house, money in the manufacturing jeweler's safe and food in Nick's Grocery Store. Life and death, pleasure and duty, riches and necessities all merge and interpenetrate as the black man gouges through cellar walls, peeks, robs, runs, faints. He builds his house in a cave. He takes "the serious toys of the men who lived" down into his sewer, hooking up a radio, pecking aimlessly on a typewriter, papering the cave walls with money (the legal tender of a "people who lived on some far-off planet"). As "the walls blaze with a yellow green fire" the man hangs a meat cleaver and wrist watches and rings as ornaments; the oozing floor is impacted with diamonds, "brittle fire." Turned out of the white man's world, the Negro turns his sewer into a sacred grotto of stolen goods, a "glorious victory." For he has learned the white man's lesson well enough to imitate it:

He sat on the chest and frowned. Maybe anything's right, he mumbled. Yes, if the world as men had made it was right, then anything else was right, any act a man took to satisfy himself. . . .

All he needs to make it complete is some white Man Friday to run his errands, keep his mansion in order.

Yet the cave walls become unbearable, and his possessions begin to have a mental life of their own. "The meat cleaver brooded." To fully imitate the white man is to go as mad. When a night watchman is brutally beaten for all the stolen

goods, the underground man has an impulse to return all
his toys. The helpless watchman blows out his brains before
the stolen goods can be returned and the policemen say,
"Our hunch was right, he was guilty. . . ." Self-destruction
proves guilt, the mad circularity of white rationalization:
because they live that way they do not deserve to live near
us, because we have made them dirty they are unclean and
their present uncleanliness proves that they were always
dirty. The underground man, sent by madness into the hole,
becomes truly mad as he lives in it. He is no longer an individual; he splits.

At the far end of the room he saw a crowd of people huddled
in a corner, afraid of his body. Though lying dead upon the
table, he was standing in some mysterious way at his side, ward-
ing off the people, guarding his body, and laughing to himself
as he observed the situation.

The final pages of the story are filled with insane laughter,
bellows from the white cops and screeches of the madman
"bursting with happiness." Emerging from his sewer he is
rejected by the prim black community in the church ("You
can't act rowdy in God's house") and the white men—the
"Lawson, Murphy, Johnson" team—that had originally
wrung his confession out of him. He learns "it was all a
mistake" and the murderer "wasn't colored at all." The
mind caves in, flying "back over the blur of the time lived
in the underground blackness." The symbols begin to grow
as Wright pushes them into the very beginning of American
Negro history. Of the policemen, the underground man
thinks "they brought me here." He becomes a forlorn slave.
And his sewer becomes for a grotesque moment the Underground Railway. The story is a nightmare of recapitulation.

The black man throws himself away into the whiteness of
the world: "He wanted to make a hymn, prance about in
physical ecstasy, throw his arm about the policemen in fel-

lowship." He becomes "a little boy playing a game" of insane love for his persecutors. It is equal to their hatred,
their insanity toward him. At the end of the story he tries
to take them down to see what he has done where they had
sent him, the transformation of the sewer into "the glittering
cave, the shouting walls, and the laughing floor." He jumps
down, knee deep in water, looks up to a pistol barrel, and
they blow his brains out. The manhole cover clangs shut
and he descends into the bowels of the planet. "You've got
to shoot his kind. They'd wreck things." He would wreck
things by living them out to the dirty end, then coming
back with the information and the madness that passes understanding.

It is not entirely accurate to speak of the story's "symbols."
We are forced to participate in the central character's mind
so utterly that the objects looming up before our eyes rarely
seem symbolic. We meet them head on. In the dim eeriness
and stench of the sewer, rat teeth chattering at our trousers,
we see a baby not just as part of the neat balancing act that
includes the corpse in the burial society. The baby is dead.
It is refuse. It bespeaks some real, nameless horror in the
upper world, some actuality that we encounter and some
terror that we cannot fully name. The energy of the story so
successfully fuses naturalistic detail and Gothic allegory that
it becomes almost hallucinatory in its effect. The ground of
meaning keeps sliding out from under us. Only when we
return, equipped for the nightmare with a separate sense
from the one we had when living through it, do the signifi-
cances begin to be clear.

A major strength of the piece is that Wright played it to
some length, seventy pages. We are caught up and participate in the action as we do in a novel, yet we perceive a
brevity and clarity of impact that we usually associate with
the short story. At the end we discover that there is no way

out; the horror is fully enforced because we have been taken all the way in.

"Man of All Work" is not the "tight, raging, diamond-hard exercise in irony," the "masterpiece," that Baldwin claimed it was in his essay "Alas, Poor Richard." The technique of telling the story entirely in dialogue gets Wright into trouble, too much "fill" and throwaway stage lines. If the story actually were mounted on a stage, the little fits of dialogue to get us over the characters' goings-in and goings-out might not be so bothersome. But on the printed page we see the physical maneuverings for what they are. Too often the dialogue is doing the job of exposition; it does not sound like dialogue but only provides information:

Now, all of our money's tied up in this house and we can't make the last two payments.

If we both hadn't lost our jobs at the same time. Giving birth knocked me out of my job. And your boss had to close his restaurant.

Nevertheless, in spite of these flaws (and a slight overplaying of the story, about five pages) "Man of All Work" is very fine, achieving at its best moments a savage hilarity. The theme is familiar: a Negro male's morale falls apart when the woman is the head of the household. As Wright tells it, the only way this man can make any fast money, in his desperate circumstances, is to become the woman. He dresses up in his wife's clothes to become a cook in the white folks' house. The masquerade is intended to last for two months, to pay their mortgage.

At the beginning the man is rather like his wife, taking care of the baby, giving it the bottle. He explains to his son, "Now, watch. I lift her head up a bit, then put the nipple in her mouth." He is a "professional cook," and since his wife is bedridden he has to do all the household duties. With his tenor voice and tiny feet, his wife's clothes and her role perfectly fit him. But the greatest assistance he will have in bringing it off will lie in the ignorance of the audience itself: "Who looks that close at us colored people anyhow?" So he is hired by the whites and becomes a pretty little Aunt Jemima: "Ha, ha!" Shaved painfully close, padded in all the right places, he becomes a hot little piece. So hot that the white Massa cannot resist a little snuggling in the kitchen. In the ensuing fight the little colored lady is shot and her manhood is discovered. But he will live— perhaps to tell the tale. To hush it all up, the white folks agree to a pay-off of two hundred dollars: now the Negro family has money to keep their house, the medical bills are covered, and at the end of the story they are crying with happiness at their success and crying with bitter shame at their degradation. The final outbursting word of the piece— "Oooouuwa!"—is pathetic, but the Man of All Work at least has a small financial success.

Wright did a brief introductory note to Jean Paul Sartre's play on race relations in the American South, "The Respectful Prostitute," when it was published in *Art and Action: A Book of Literature, the Arts, and Civil Liberties* (the tenth anniversary issue of *Twice a Year*). Wright said it was important to see Sartre's play not as a "satire" but as a "farce." In "Man of All Work," Wright is trying a medium he had never worked before, the "farce," and he brings it off with great skill. When the child warns, "Papa is quick and strong," the new maid mutters, "I can outrun him." When the maid responds to the sexual assault, slugging the father across the kitchen floor, the wide-eyed child pipes, "Don't kill Papa, Lucy!" And at the very end when the Man of All Work is brought home on a stretcher, and his wife asks where her dress is, he can only mumble, "Oh, I don't know.

I lost it—" The insanity of the situation is embodied in the exchanges between the characters. The story is "hilarious" in both senses of that word: outrageously, exhaustingly funny, "Man of All Work" is also laughter at the point of utter desperation and nervous collapse.

The finest scene occurs when the white mistress calls from the bathtub, asking the new maid to come scrub her back. Perhaps Richard Wright could not have more fully enjoyed —simply enjoyed—writing any other scene. Here was a major confrontation in his life's work: the black male and the white woman. But this time with a difference. It is a long scene, and Wright must have fallen away from his typewriter more than once as he protracted its deliciousness, tantalizing us with each new detail, pushing it all into unbearable comedy. When one reads this late story, Wright's heroes—Big Boy and Bigger Thomas and Jake Jackson and Cross Damon and Fishbelly and their cronies—all pass in review in our minds as we see them now, in drag, staring at the white nude body in the bath. Here is the benediction, the laughter issuing out to black boys, retrieving them:

—Lucy!
—Yessum. Where are you, Mrs. Fairchild?
—I'm here in the bathroom. Won't you come in? I want you to wash my back.
—Hunh?

The "hunh?" is exactly right. We see him/her suddenly stop in the room, breath blown and eyes bugging. The gradual entry into the bathroom ("Lucy? Why are you poking your head like that around the door?") is slowly pulled out, so that we can watch Carl-Lucy turning to rubber, sweating, ineffectually daubing at the expanse of white sudsy flesh. The white woman stands dripping, asks for a towel, and shrieks: "WHAT IS HAPPENING TO YOU, LUCY?" But poor Lucy recovers himself and obeys. The mistress wants to sit and chat, "to talk frankly as one woman to another." Wright cannot resist playing it all the way, making the plump naked white woman primp and pose, asking her new maid, in the single funniest line of the story: "My breasts—aren't they much too large?" The black man reels. The mind blinks off. "Maybe . . . a little . . ." When at last Carl-Lucy is free to go out he totters to the back porch. The child, "Lily"-white, asks why her Lucy is sweating; the reply is a comic epitaph to Wright's work: "It was hot there in that bathroom."

Near the beginning of his story, Bigger Thomas had asked, "It's funny how the white folks treat us, ain't it?" His pal, Gus, replied, "It better be funny." And in "Man of All Work" Wright was retelling the dilemma of all his native sons: it better be funny, and it is—funny, obscenely funny, the dirtiest practical joke a culture can play on its people. The black man from Natchez, who had confessed that he never could seem to tell a joke, achieved one at the end. From across the seas the last word of Black Boy was most clear as a gale of sardonic laughter.

CHAPTER 7

The Ordeal by Fire

Black Boy begins with a young boy, so wearied of boredom that to get relief he has to start a fire. In the ghettos of the 1960's the long summer tedium of nothing to do, of being hot and cramped, is broken by an idea: burn the place down. It is something to do. And when Sargent Shriver addresses a Senate hearing, he knows the war on poverty is "looked upon as some sort of a fire brigade operation." The flames of our destroyed cities light up the flames at the heart of Richard Wright's work. He knew it began in fire and he was afraid that it ultimately might be fought out in fire.

One of his early poems, published in *Midland Left* (February 1935), is titled "Obsession." Preceding almost all his work,

175

it could be used as a summary of it; Wright saw at the very beginning where he would have to go:

> Yet again I must speak of it
> Yet again I must speak of it
> For it has grown to an obsession
> Become the pivot-point
> Of my days and hours . . .
> This haunting American symbol
> Of fire cooking human flesh
> The dreadful flame that will not die
> Has dwarfed and paled all other symbols . . .

"The dreadful flame" would curl up all through his life and work, from the beginning when he burned down the family house to the very end when in Paris, on the last day of November in 1960, his remains were cremated and set in the Cimetière du Père Lachaise. His mind was constantly turning to fire, that image dwarfing and paling all other symbols. So often his verbs are variations on "burn," and "flame," and "blaze," and "kindle." Fire—and its complementing element, water—appear together in *Uncle Tom's Children*: Brother Mann is killed by flood in "Down by the Riverside"; in the following story, "Long Black Song," Silas is consumed by fire. Bigger Thomas puts white womanhood in the furnace, and white manhood floods him off the roof with a fire hose. Big Boy's pal is roasted alive; the murder of the Fascist and the Communist in *The Outsider* takes place in the light of a leaping fire; in Fishbelly's story the central event is the burning of the whore house.

Gaston Bachelard has written in *The Psychoanalysis of Fire* that "on several occasions the creation of fire is associated with an act of violence: fire is the objective phenomenon of an inner rage. . . ." Wright's prose is the expression of that "inner rage" compelling him to speak; the torrential violence that occurs so often in his work is accompanied almost always by scenes of fire. The language often takes on a Biblical quality; when Bigger roars out of bed at the beginning of Part II he thinks he had "put her body in the fiery furnace." Fires are linked with Christian faith, as on the burning cross of the Ku Klux Klan. And when Dan Taylor in "Fire and Cloud" speaks to his congregation he can say:

Ah know whut yo life is! Ah done felt it! Its *fire*. Its sufferin! Its hell!

Hell-fire is the image that embodies the Negro's place of residence in America, the ghetto of endless burning. In that underworld all human action is contorted into single flames, parts of the endless surrounding fire.

Fire springs from a sexual rage and pours into the violence of sexual torment. In "Big Boy Leaves Home" Bobo is burned to death in a scene suggestive of perverse sexuality. Bigger burns Mary's body in an act of symbolic rape, and the prosecutor in the courtroom takes the burning as evidence that there had been a literal rape. In the stories of Bigger, Silas, Bobo, Fishbelly, and Cross Damon, the sexuality and fire are joined. Bachelard writes that "it is the fire which can 'open bodies' " and "this 'opening' of bodies, this possession of bodies from within, this *total* possession, is sometimes an obvious sexual act. It is performed . . . with the Rod of Fire." The sexuality that has been choked off, the unpossessed desires of a people, are expressed in this act of, as Bachelard emphasizes, "*total* possession."

Fire becomes, finally, an act of "knowledge." The desire to open bodies is (the pun traditionally carried in the verb "to know") engendering power. It is the "flaming minister" that Shakespeare's great black man speaks of when he cries out for "Promethean heat." To have the fire is to have the secret, the knowledge of full manhood. It is to possess the secret thing of the gods, to steal and have on earth their power.

In *Black Boy* Richard is taken by his mother to see the father who has abandoned them. In the scene, the fire appears with all its connotations: "I found myself standing in a room in a frame house. My father and a strange woman were sitting before a bright fire that blazed in a grate." The boy senses some great loss, some sexual disorder, and he impulsively seeks its meaning in the fire. When his father calls to him, "I backed away, shaking my head, keeping my eyes on the fire." All the mysteries of the confrontation seem to the boy to be there in the hearth, if he can only understand what the fire means. "I looked at my mother, at the strange woman, at my father, then into the fire." The boy and his mother are defeated once again, and Richard goes home to think.

Many times in the years after that the image of my father and the strange woman, their faces lit by the dancing flames, would surge up in my imagination so vivid and strong that I felt I could reach out and touch it; I would stare at it, feeling that it possessed some vital meaning which always eluded me.

To become fully free is to come into possession of the fire. And Wright discovered that his freedom would have to be through the fire itself; only by entering into it could he open the body of his suffering to intelligence. He concludes the first chapter of *Black Boy* with the image of being lifted in "burning arms" to "knowing." When he left the house of his father and the woman, Richard said he "had the feeling that I had had to do with something unclean." Fire is a way of burning all the dirt and waste away. The legendary figure of Empedocles sought to cleanse himself in the fires of Mount Etna and left us his *Purifications*. Wright's work is a sustained attempt to lift the fires of his life into the mind; "the numbness might thaw out and let me feel the pain." It is an effort to fight fire with fire, a sacred art of kindling and a desperate gamble.

II

Native Son has been the touchstone of this study because that book embodies the story that Richard Wright was telling over and over again throughout his fiction. *Black Boy* is more perfect, fully controlled, but *Native Son* represents the characters, situations, and details that Wright had already worked with in *Lawd Today* and "Big Boy Leaves Home" and to which he would return in *The Outsider, The Long Dream,* and various shorter pieces. The story in all these works is essentially one story, Richard Wright's controlling myth.

It begins with a group of young black pals, lazily moving along, joking, laughing, at ease. In the warm male camaraderie a fight breaks out in which one of the boys distinguishes himself by brute power. That strength is then directed toward "the white folks." Almost always the group of pals is four: three friends accompany Bigger Thomas, Cross Damon, Big Boy, Jake Jackson, Fishbelly. Their friendship begins the book (and, Wright confessed in "How Bigger Was Born," "the actual writing of the book began with the scene in the pool room" and only after the first draft was done did he decide to insert the symbolic rat).

The second major ingredient of the myth is the sexual confrontation between the black man (who distinguished himself in the fight with his pals) and a young, attractive white woman. That confrontation occurs in a place where there is explicitly a No Trespassing sign (as with Fishbelly) or an understanding that the area is off limits (as in "Big Boy Leaves Home") or where the taboos of American culture have for centuries been warning the Negro he cannot enter (as in *Native Son*). It is a scene of extraordinary violence and usually results in death. It fulfills a curse that earlier in the story had been outlined, a prophecy come true, as in "The Man Who Lived Underground" or Bigger's sense that "something awful's goin to happen to me" and "I knew that some time or other they was goin to get me" or Fishbelly's feeling when caught in the room with the white girl that "he had been waiting for something like this to happen to him all of his life." In the confrontation either the black man or the white woman is naked (or partially undressed), as in "Big Boy Leaves Home," "The Man Who Killed a Shadow," and "Man of All Work." Or, as in *Native Son* and *The Long Dream,* the white woman is in a bedroom.

The confrontation involves a scene of fire: Mary Dalton in the furnace, Bobo at the stake, the inferno in *The Long Dream,* the fight to the death in the light from the apartment fireplace in *The Outsider.* The fire is carried on in the reprisals visited on the black community by the white as crosses are burned, houses consumed, bodies cooked. These reprisals bring together in violence the two worlds that at the beginning of the story are so carefully separated.

The minds of the black men are filled with dreams of great mobility and power. In "Big Boy Leaves Home" the chums play at being engineers on great trains, constantly calling directions to each other at the beginning, and as children they played in great kilns which represent locomotives. Fishbelly constantly dreams of great engines driving down long tracks. Both Jake Jackson and Bigger Thomas attend movies about aviators and dream of being able to fly like "them white boys." They want to be great destructive pilots, dropping bombs on the white world, and flying home to a pretty girl. Frantz Fanon writes in *The Wretched of the Earth* that

the first thing which the native learns is to stay in his place, and not to go beyond certain limits. This is why the dreams of the native are always of muscular prowess; his dreams are of action and of aggression. I dream I am jumping, swimming, running, climbing; I dream that I burst out laughing, that I span a river in one stride.

Wright's heroes are constantly dreaming in these terms: Jake Jackson's story begins with his early morning dream of stairs and stairs and stairs, roaring up them; several of Fishbelly's dreams involve great hurtling motion, as do Big Boy's; and Bigger dreams of flying. In the stage version of *Native Son,* Bigger cries out his vision in the terms that Fanon would later use: "I wanted to be free to walk wild and free with steps a mile long—over the houses, over the rivers, and straddling the mountains and on. . . ."

But the dream of mobility usually ends in a nightmare of flight. Bigger, Big Boy, Fishbelly, Jake, the Man Who Lived Underground, the Man Who Killed a Shadow, Dave Saunders, Cross Damon—all run frantically for their lives.

These are the weapons in Wright's arsenal: the opening group of pals, the sexual confrontation between the races in a forbidden place, the murder and fires, mass retaliation by whites on a helpless black community, dreams of mobility and terrors of frantic flight, torrential storms, all of which unfold a curse that is articulated at the beginning: it all was going to happen some day.

In "How Bigger Was Born," Wright says that he was trying to achieve a theatrical effect. That effect was an important part of his story, and Baldwin later quoted Wright on the reason for its importance:

Almost all Negroes, as Richard once pointed out, are almost always acting, but before a white audience—which is quite incapable of judging their performance: and even a "bad nigger" is, inevitably, giving something of a performance, even if the entire purpose of his performance is to terrify or blackmail white people.

Wright indicated that his "bad nigger" was a "dramatic" figure; in "How Bigger Was Born" he said, "I kept out of the story as much as possible, for I wanted the reader to feel that there was nothing between him and Bigger; that the story was a special *première* given in his own private theatre."

When, with Paul Green, Wright mounted *Native Son* on Broadway (with Orson Welles in charge of production) he discovered that a stage play would lose one great advantage of the novel: we could not get inside Bigger's mind. We could only observe the outward signs, the consequences of his terror; we could not share it, could not feel it registering in the skull. There is an important, an essential, disparity in the novel between feelings and act. We watch Bigger "act" for the white people while at the same time we participate in all his inner rage and fear that he covers up so that the white people cannot see. On the stage, with Bigger up there, away from us, we lose this essential perspective. And since one of the major achievements of the novel had been Wright's ability to immerse us so completely in Bigger's way of feeling, a major dimension had to be cut away. It was perhaps for that reason that Wright and Green "cleaned up" Bigger, made him less of a monster. Bigger does not kill Clara (Bessie, in the novel). She is in front of him when the police come: "her arms go up and about him in an impulsive gesture of love. Another shot rings out and she sags down in his arms."

The story of *Native Son* was more successfully mounted on the stage in another form, by another man; the formal mastery of the subject shows how the author was able to go beyond Wright in many ways, and in its central scene and a variety of details it shows how much the author owed to Wright. In October of 1959—the year before Wright's death —in Paris, where Wright was living, Jean Genet's play *The Blacks* was first performed.

In the printed text of the play, Genet says that his work "is intended for a white audience," but if it is ever performed before a black audience, then a white person, male or female, should be invited every evening. The organizer of the show should welcome him formally, dress him in ceremonial costume and lead him to his seat, preferably in the front row of the orchestra. The actors will play for him. A spotlight should be focused upon this symbolic white throughout the performance.

The play is an act of assault upon its audience. It attacks the white world. Genet says that if no whites will come, then black spectators must wear white masks; if the black audience refuses the masks, then a dummy should be used. The meaning of the play is inextricable from its performance situation, its formal consciousness of spectators. This play about blacks murdering a white is itself trying to accomplish, in the act of performance, a kind of murder in the mind, the mind of the white in the audience. When Eugene Ionesco walked out on the play he was reacting intelligently; to the reporter who asked why he had left, Ionesco replied, "Because I am white."

There are entirely too many traces of *Native Son* in *The Blacks* to assume that Genet was not consciously and carefully working with Wright's book. There are so many direct echoes we must conclude that the novel itself was Genet's source, and not talk about it, or the stage version of Wright and Green (which played in Paris) or the movie version in which Wright impersonated Bigger. Only in the novel are all the ingredients present which we find in Genet's play.

When the curtain is drawn, the Blacks are gathered around the casket of a white woman. A central character, Archibald Absalom Wellington, tells us:

Tonight, our sole concern will be to entertain you. So we have killed this white woman. There she lies. Only *we* could have done it the way we did it—savagely.

The murderer was a character named Village. Just as Bigger Thomas had cringed in shame because of the humiliating questions Mary Dalton had kept asking him, so Village asks of the blacks around him: "Do you want a detailed description of the humiliations she made me feel?" Mary Dalton in *Native Son* had been unable to scream, drunk, half-asleep, in her dark bedroom, then with Bigger holding a pillow over her face. In *The Blacks* Village says that the white girl in her bedroom did not scream: "She was dozing. She half awoke. The blackness of the night . . ." Village tells us "she reeked" of liquor and "I strangled her." Mary Dalton had jerked up, stiffened, and then collapsed. Village says, "She stiffened a bit . . . then she had a spasm, and that was that." Bigger Thomas had carried Mary Dalton downstairs in a trunk; Village says that he carried the white girl away in a crate. Bigger put Mary into the furnace; a character named the "Governor" cries out in Genet's play: "They're going to cook her. . . ." Bigger carries his revolver with him, and threatens Jan with it; Village says he had no "trouble on the way back" because "I had this" and shows a revolver. Bigger had always wanted to murder; Village says, "It's always murder that we dream about."

Later in Genet's play, when the characters go over the murder again, we encounter new details that come from *Native Son*. Village says, "From the attic where her bed was, I could hear her mother calling for her evening medicine." Bigger kills Mary Dalton in a high room of the house when her mother comes in, a mother stricken with blindness. Village asked "for another glass of rum"; it is a bottle of "rum" that Jan and Mary share with Bigger. Village tells us that "snow was falling on the town"; Bigger sees from the window that snow is falling on Chicago. In the basement of the Dalton home, when Bigger beheads Mary, he touches the knife to her throat and finds that he cannot cut hard enough, must abandon the knife for a hatchet. In Genet's play, Village speaks of "the resistance of the flesh to the knife." And just as Bigger put Mary "into the fiery furnace" so Village says "she even roasted in the flames."

When Bigger kills, he kills out of terror and hatred of the white world represented in "the white blur floating toward him." The Judge in *The Blacks* says Village "killed out of hatred. Hatred of the color white." And by his act of murder Bigger feels a sense of freedom: "He had murdered and had created a new life for himself." Archibald cries out to the blacks: *"We'll* be saved by *that,"* and points to the catafalque. Later he repeats: "His crime saves him." Wright had said, "His crime was an anchor weighing him safely. . . ." *The Blacks* and *Native Son* locate in murder the act of liberation, calling up the cursed thing as an act of survival.

Yet the murder of the white girl, in Genet's play, is always a performance—not only the "performance" we see, but the "performance" the actors themselves see. And Archibald cries out to the blacks impersonating the white power, after the murder, "Keep your masks on!" The man who as actor kills the white girl is also involved in the great revolution going on offstage. Archibald says, "It's no longer a matter of staging a performance." The actor is also "a real man." And Newport News cries

But though we can put on an act in front of them [pointing to the audience], we've got to stop acting when we're among ourselves. We'll have to get used to taking responsibility for blood—our own. And the moral weight . . .

The performance of Genet's play involves an endless series of reflecting mirrors, where the performance itself is an observance of a performance by those who themselves are "performing" a political deed off stage. At one point the acting out of the murder on stage is called "a farewell performance"; it is a farewell performance to the old image of The Blacks, who are also getting on to other murders, other identities.

If, then, a dozen details in the central event of the play, the presentation of it, and the notations of the murder all show that Genet is deeply in debt to Wright, the ultimate significance Genet draws from them and the artistic integrity of his work, its formal plan and its language, show how Genet was able to go beyond Wright. *The Blacks* is a "clown show"; it manages to be both that and, quite literally, a "black mass." It is a sacred ritual, a holy communion of black souls. The way out of their imprisoning metaphor is accomplished in their act of embodying that metaphor as a reality. "We are what they want us to be. We shall therefore be it to the very end, absurdly."

In the dialogue of the play, the actors continually remind themselves of the symbolic role that they are playing, for us and for themselves. The challenge to the mind is to remember that the stereotypic metaphor is exactly that, a horrid figure of our cultural speech. Genet criticizes and controls that metaphor in the careful ritualization of the entire action (the masks, the ceremonial gestures, the "playing" to the audience itself an act of ceremony). Archibald says, "We shall increase the distance that separates us—a distance that is basic—by our pomp, our manners, our insolence—for we are also actors." The "distance that is basic" is the point of the *clownerie*:

What's left for us? The theater! We'll play at being reflected in it, and we'll see ourselves—big black narcissists—slowly disappearing into its waters.

And when Village complains that he does not want to disappear, Archibald says, "Nothing will remain of you but the foam of your rage. Since they merge us with an image and drown us in it, let the image set their teeth on edge!"

In 1938 Richard Wright was setting out to do a book that would "set their teeth on edge." In an interview with a reporter for the *Daily Worker* ("An Author Discusses His Craft," December 13, 1938), Wright said something about his novel which tells us more than "How Bigger Was Born" about his ultimate aim:

"The chief character is drawn into committing a crime . . . oh, what a crime!" Dick drew his head between his shoulders, shelteringly, and chuckled. . . .

And in "How Bigger Was Born" he says:

Like Bigger himself, I felt a mental censor—product of the fears which a Negro feels from living in America—standing over me, draped in white, warning me not to write.

Richard Wright "like Bigger himself" is in a room with his secret guilt, terrified by the figure "draped in white." The act of writing involves becoming as completely *black* as he can be, the elevation of his own blackness into frontal consciousness. The terms of the curse being exorcised had been so personally unbearable that to attack the cultural mind meant also to attack one's own mind. If, in all his writing life, Richard Wright was playing with fire, he would have to get burned. The great accomplishment of *Native Son* is the sheer energy with which Wright makes us feel Bigger's ordeal. To accumulate the force, Wright was in some ways crippled by it; to know the cruelty, to separate from the scores of meaningless tortures the few that could stand for them all, is also to be so deeply hurt that for Wright a full recovery was perhaps impossible. He takes us into the nightmare he had lived; he knows it as well as he knows the color of his skin.

In "How Bigger Was Born" he presents in his figure of

Bigger 4 a rebellious spirit always fighting to keep his dignity under Jim Crow, always complaining "the white folks won't let us do nothing," and always reading books. He is something like the young Richard of *Black Boy*. And, Wright says, this Bigger 4 ended in an asylum for the insane. In his essay Wright will say, "Like Bigger himself, I . . ." or cringe in italics: "for a moment I'd allow myself, vicariously, to feel as Bigger felt—not much, just a little, just a *little*—but, still, there it was."

But, still, there it was. And how, Richard Wright asked in 1938, could he avoid the fate of Bigger 4? If he saw too clearly, like that wretched boy, his mind could fall out. In the last section of the novel, a helpless lunatic is brought into Bigger's cell block. Why is he crazy? When he is shoved into Bigger's cell, we can see Wright's horrified consciousness that the boy could be himself, going into the cell with the "bad nigger" he has created. Writhing and screaming, the young man asks for his "papers," his writing, his "evidence." A policeman says the young man thinks "he's got to the bottom of why colored folks are treated bad and he's going to tell. . . ." Wright himself was claiming to tell no more, no less. The young man in the cell block is crazy because he believed too much that he would be listened to, and he saw too much what the real damage had been. Wright presents this demented creature as the voice of reason ruined by its trusting attachment to the truth, the voice echoing in the chambers of our house of detention.

Bigger himself picks up the substance of the madman's cries. At the very end of the story Bigger complains that Max's questions "made me think and thinking's made me scared a little. . . ." Bigger's fear is sometimes presented in terms which seem to describe not Bigger's mentality but Richard Wright's. In the opening pages we are told that Bigger has in his eyes a pensive, brooding amusement, as of a man who had been long confronted and tantalized by a riddle whose answer seemed always just on the verge of escaping him, but prodding him irresistibly on to seek its solution.

Bigger, as we see him in the first section of the book, is not capable of "pensive brooding"; Richard Wright, as we see him throughout his career, is just such a man. In all the versions of his native son that he would create he seems to be "long confronted and tantalized by a riddle"; his novels and short stories record how he was always searching for the answer which "seemed always just on the verge of escaping him, but prodding him irresistibly on."

The crucial difference between *Native Son* and *The Blacks* is one of distance. *Native Son* is in many ways an unaccomplished work. While Wright continually drives to recognize that the crime is in the "head," the architecture of the book is seriously weakened by his inability in the final section to follow fully the implications of his central image and his lack of care in the prose. Genet's subsequent achievement in *The Blacks* was to poise the curse, to see it finally and in artistic integrity from the outside; Wright's genius was to see it totally from within. Wright said that for Bigger, "the moment he allowed what his life meant to enter fully into his consciousness, he would either kill himself or someone else." Everywhere in *Native Son*—where Wright is at his best and where he is at his worst—we feel his agonized knowledge of that horror.

III

The question of how a "Negro writer" becomes a "writer" is an old one, and it has not often stimulated answers that go beyond condescension and platitude. Richard Gibson (in the *Kenyon Review,* No. 13, 1951) claimed that the Negro writer is, in one way or another, "trapped by the Problem." Gibson's "professional liberals" only want to read books by those Negroes who know their place and are content to spend their literary energy "picking away industriously at the great problem." Gibson says this "professional liberal" is a sour little person who thinks the Negro writer "must be kept his pet, to be protected at the end of a leash." What is needed, Gibson says, "is not another Negro Writer but a writer who happens also to be a Negro." That such a creature could be born was the hope of Herbert Hill when he introduced, more than a decade after Gibson's manifesto, his anthology *Soon One Morning* (a volume dedicated to Wright's memory). Hill said that the contemporary black writer was beginning to see that he had "to break through the limits of racial parochialism into the whole range of the modern writer's preoccupations." Hill sees a more fully controlled, more ambitious literature "as the Negro writer moves beyond anger" and "refuses to be limited to racial protest." We have come to the time when "self-pity and dreary rage are clearly no longer enough."

But no writer, no man, in America "happens" to be a Negro. Richard Wright could only wince when Gertrude Stein tried to tell him that he wrote as a man, not as a Negro. Wright made Negroness his cultural community, and it defined his area of consciousness. When he speaks as a black man about his America, he means the most and his voice carries greatest authority. In his essay on "The Literature of the Negro in the United States" he speaks of how European writers like Dumas and Pushkin (who happened to be Negroes) were at home in the idioms and scenes of the dominant culture. But for himself, writing in America,

being a Negro has to do with the American scene, with race hate, rejection, ignorance, segregation, discrimination, slavery, murder, fiery crosses, and fear.

In "The Man Who Went to Chicago" he describes the Negro he met on the slum streets as a man "held at bay by the hate of others, preoccupied with his own feelings, continuously at war with reality." That phrase, "continuously at war with reality," recurs in Wright's work as his recognition that the social and psychological pressures exerted on him as a man are unavoidably there, operating on him as a writer. His intelligence, his reflexes, his tensions do not disappear when he sits down to write. If he tries to write "colorlessly" he probably will do exactly that, separated from his deepest energies. But writing as the man he is—black—he is constantly in the "ancient agonies."

Agonies ancient and unrelenting. If the history of American culture since *Native Son* has proved anything, it has shown that to be a black writer in America does not involve a lessening of rage. The portrait that Boris Max draws of Bigger in the courtroom reappears stroke for stroke in the portrait of "the typical rioter" of 1967 in the *Report of the National Advisory Commission on Civil Disorders*—"a teenager or young adult" who has dropped out of school, who is "employed in a menial low-status job not because of lack of training, ability, or ambition, but because of discrimination by employers," who is "extremely hostile to whites" and "highly distrustful of the political system." Boris Max's Bigger of 1940 can be seen in the Kerner Commission's image of the young black man of the late 1960's: "a time-bomb ticking in the heart of the richest nation in the history of the world." Robert Coles, in an article "When the Southern Negro Moves North" (New York *Times Magazine*, September 17, 1967), quotes a Negro mother on her son: " 'He's all mixed up. One minute he tells me he wants to be a policeman and he'd shoot down all the niggers who tried to cause trouble. Then the next minute he says he's going to kill a white man one day, he just knows it, and when he does it'll be about time.' " Three decades gone, and it is still Bigger. When Coles asks today's young ghetto dweller what he wants to be, the answer is: "Maybe a pilot, or a president of something. . . ." That again is Bigger, wanting to fly, playing president of the country or of the corporation. The young black man says to Dr. Coles that whatever happens he has at least got to have a start with "something even half good, even half good; something that I can hold in my hands and know it'll stay there." And, as with *Native Son,* when he realizes that the system is going to keep his hand empty, he finally must fill it with a weapon.

Bigger Thomas is our contemporary; what Carmichael and Hamilton call "institutional racism" has persisted with crushing force to keep him in our streets. Bigger lives, and the legacy of Richard Wright involves for the black writer the question of how his world can be presented in challenging terms that are as electric and viable today as were Wright's in his time. When in *Anger and Beyond* Mr. Hill says that "self-pity and dreary rage are clearly no longer enough," one can only ask if they ever had been. That great "modern writer" Hill speaks of simply does not exist, is not separate from his cultural identity. Hill is surely right to object that the black writer must not confine himself to the language of propaganda, but he speaks as if cultural identity could be defined only by that language. The enterprise is not to break out of "the narrow compartment reserved for Negro writers" but rather to take full measure of that compartment, to decorate it, to make a black castle of the white cage, and move on to a liberating independence of self-definition.

In that effort, the definitions of Richard Wright hold an important place. James Baldwin confessed that for him Wright became "alas! my father," and the son has copied leaves in his father's book. In "The Harlem Ghetto" Baldwin writes that in every act of violence, particularly violence against white men, Negroes feel a certain thrill of identification, a wish to have done it themselves, a feeling that old scores are being settled at last.

Wright says that Bigger Thomas felt, after the murder of Mary Dalton, "like a man who had been somehow cheated, but had now evened the score." Jean Paul Sartre's diagnosis of the black man's "impulse to murder" as "the expression of the natives' collective unconscious" is another way of saying what Baldwin meant by asserting in "Many Thousands Gone" that no Negro in America is able to escape the "Bigger Thomas in the skull." Baldwin says:

there is, I should think, no Negro living in America who has not felt, briefly or for long periods, with anguish sharp or dull, in varying degrees and to varying effect, simple, naked and unanswerable hatred; who has not wanted to smash any white face he may encounter in a day, to violate, out of motives of the cruelest vengeance, their women, to break the bodies of all white people and to bring them low, as low as that dust into which he himself has been and is being trampled; no Negro, finally, who has not had to make his own precarious adjustment to the "nigger" who surrounds him and to the "nigger" in himself.

Again, Baldwin looks to his "father," who had said in "How Bigger Was Born" that Bigger's relationship to the white world is a "relationship whose effects are carried by every Negro, like scars, somewhere in his body and mind."

Wright wrote in his Paris diary that "the next great area of discovery in the Negro will be the dark landscape of his own mind. . . ." The idea that he could be the "spiritual father" of those setting out on this "next great area of discovery" was not altogether pleasant for Richard Wright, as when Baldwin claimed his paternity (and whenever the name Baldwin came up, Chester Himes could drive Wright to exasperation by calling him "Big Daddy"). But Wright is the father of the contemporary black writer because when we come to Wright's best work we are faced with the central question about being black in America. Richard Wright was the first man to put it to us with all its naked power. In *Soul on Ice* Eldridge Cleaver remarks that he washed his hands "in the blood of the martyr, Malcolm X, whose retreat from the precipice of madness created new room for others to turn about in, and now I am caught up in that tiny space, attempting a maneuver of my own." Wright, for black writers, did something of the same thing—as Cleaver acknowledges in his tribute to Wright as "supreme for his profound political, economic, and social reference." Wright opened room for others by himself going to the edge. To be sure, he began and to a certain clear extent remained a Marxist of the thirties; he is of his time. He wrote in terms that are not altogether applicable to this present—a present which is still excruciatingly barbaric, crude on our streets, and yet in careful minds so complexly threatening and tortuously subtle. We live on a frontier and in a honeycomb, whereas Wright's work inhabits mainly the frontier. While the situation he wrote about persists with a furious sameness, the ways of understanding that situation have radically changed. But the farther we get from Richard Wright and his modes of thought, the better we can see the extent of the debt we owe him and the integrity of his own achievements. He continues to be with us—as the figure of Harry Ames in John A. Williams's *The Man Who Cried I Am,* as a Caesar to Baldwin's Brutus (when Cleaver casts himself as Mark Antony), as the man who made the major breakthrough into modern territory. However outmoded some of his weapons may seem now, Richard Wright was the man who first conquered the big ground.

In a speech given in November of 1960 Wright quoted what Robert Park, the sociologist, had asked him twenty years previously: "How in hell did you happen?" That is the question. For Richard Wright America was not the name of a country; it was the name of a mental sickness. But an unhappy, violent childhood does not necessarily create a writer whose work consistently expresses rage; it could just as possibly lead to docility, a constant effort to avoid violence, a desperately calculated serenity. Wright's violence is part of a lifelong ordeal of violence, but it is also a determination as a writer to make sense of that experience. His best work begins somewhere beyond the bearable: it posits and explores a historical brutality embodied in a helpless boy who goes through the frenzied motions of living. Convinced that "the Negro is America's metaphor," Wright explored the American mind with the equipment America had forced him to bear in his. His work is an example of what Sartre defined as genius—"not a gift but the way out that one invents in desperate cases."

Late in his life Wright said: "Theme for Negro writers will emerge when they have begun to feel the meaning of their history as a race as though they in one lifetime had lived it themselves throughout all the long centuries." The achievement of Richard Wright came from his determined ability to explore his own individual suffering and create from it crucial examples of what "all the long centuries" mean.

INDEX

197

Blacks, The (Genet), 182–187, 189
"Blueprint for Negro Literature," 53
Bobo ("Big Boy Leaves Home"), 36, 37, 38, 84, 177, 180
Bone, Robert A., 155
Book-of-the-Month Club, 14, 64
"Bright and Morning Star," 23–24, 26–27, 77, 88
Browder, Earl, 61
Brown, Claude, 84, 134
Bruce, Lenny, 86
Burns, Ben, 65
Butcher, Margaret, 90

Canfield, Cass, 64
Carmichael, Stokely, 32, 192
Cherne, Leo, 61
Chicago, 4, 15, 17, 18, 39, 47, 58, 69, 80, 106, 152, 156, 159
Chicago *Daily Tribune*, 5–6, 17, 70, 80
Chips Are Down, The (Sartre), 150
Civil Rights Movement, 6, 7, 164
Clansman, The (Dixon), 87n
Cleaver, Eldridge, 84, 110, 132, 194
Cohn, David L., 65
Coles, Robert, 191–192
Color Curtain: A Report on the Bandung Conference, The, 141, 143, 145, 151
Communism, 29, 32, 51–52, 58–59
Communist Party, 9, 28, 34–35, 45–62, 90, 101, 138, 163, 164
Communists, 8, 33, 45, 53–54, 59, 86
Coronet, 59
Crisis, 32, 149
Cross-Currents, 52
Cross Section, 1944, 166
Cross Section, 1945, 137
Crucible, The (Miller), 110
Cullen, Countee, 144

"Daddy Goodness" (Sapin), 166
Daiches, David, 73
Daily Worker, 26, 28, 29, 46–47, 48, 50, 58, 94, 187
Dalton, Mary (*Native Son*), 64, 71, 73, 75, 83, 86, 87, 88, 96, 177, 180, 184–185, 193
Dalton, Mr. (*Native Son*), 71, 89, 93, 94
Dalton, Mrs. (*Native Son*), 87, 94
Damon, Cross (*The Outsider*), 49, 150, 152, 153–154, 173, 177, 179, 181
Daniels, Jonathan, 65
Davis, David B., 87n
Davis, Frank M., 32
Death in the Family, A (Agee), 122
Dixon, Thomas, 87n
Dostoevsky, Feodor, 64, 150, 166
"Down by the Riverside," 26, 32, 36, 176
Dreiser, Theodore, 58, 67, 68, 69
Du Bois, W. E. B., 116, 127, 128
Duffus, R. L., 137

"Early Days in Chicago," 137, 163, 164–165
Ebony, 137, 138, 160
Eight Men, 156, 165–174
Eliot, T. S., 51
Ellison, Ralph, 8, 10–13, 14, 17, 48, 116, 117–118, 119, 128, 167
Embree, E. R., 66
Empedocles, 178
Erikson, Erik, 97, 114
Esquire, 165
"Ethics of Living Jim Crow, The," 23, 50–51, 103

Fadiman, Clifton, 67
Fanon, Frantz, 21, 79, 96, 99, 100, 102, 144–145, 180, 181
Fast, Howard, 56
Federal Writers' Projects, 23, 103

80816

DATE DUE